LIVING
BEYOND
—THE—
DREAM

Praise for *Living beyond the Dream*

"Jarrod Polson is Kentucky basketball. A boy who turned down scholarships to other Division 1 schools to live out his dream of playing for the Wildcats. A dream thousands of Kentucky boys have had all over the Commonwealth. He was given little chance of playing, having to compete against the annual #1 recruiting classes of John Calipari. But not only did he play, he was an integral part of UK's 2012 National Championship. However, to me there is something more important. Jarrod Polson lives what he believes."

—CAMERON MILLS

"During the months following UK's miraculous run in the 2014 NCAA Tournament, Jarrod Polson and I were given the opportunity to visit thousands of elementary and middle school kids throughout the state of Kentucky. Those kids saw that a UK National Champion who got to live his dream can be humble, patient, and kind and still be a champion. You will love getting to know him and Him through Polson's book *Living beyond the Dream*."

—JEFF SHEPPARD

"In my time here at Kentucky, I've been fortunate to have been around some of the strongest character kids in the country. JP is at the top of that list, his faith in how he lives his life, his dedication to team and winning spirit made it fun and a joy to coach. He will always be one of my favorite wildcats."

—KENNY PAYNE

"Jarrod Polson writes about the honor to wear a Kentucky uniform and the thrill of being a part of BBN."

—DICK VITALE

LIVING BEYOND —THE— DREAM

A Journey of Faith
into the Talented World of
Kentucky Basketball

JARROD POLSON AND **WES COKER**

WESTBOW°
PRESS
A DIVISION OF THOMAS NELSON
& ZONDERVAN

WestBow Press books may be ordered through booksellers or by contacting:

WestBow Press
A Division of Thomas Nelson & Zondervan
1663 Liberty Drive
Bloomington, IN 47403
www.westbowpress.com
1 (866) 928-1240

Cover Image Credit: Allen Warford

ISBN: 978-1-4908-7112-7 (sc)
ISBN: 978-1-4908-7113-4 (e)

Library of Congress Control Number: 2015903410

Print information available on the last page.

WestBow Press rev. date: 03/27/2015

About the Authors

I taught Jarrod everything I know. If you don't believe me, watch any of our home videos. You'll witness some sort of competition between Wes, me, and Jarrod—with four years between each of us—you'll hear our mom or dad narrating, and you'll see Ashley and Alyse doing whatever it is little girls do. Most of the videos consist of me making an idiot of myself because winning was, and sadly sometimes still is, more important to me than anything. I showed Jarrod no mercy, even if it meant arguing, diving for a loose ball, or using brute force on my much smaller younger brother. It didn't matter if it was basketball, Ping-Pong, or Monopoly Jr; if there was competition, it had my name on it. I once

Photo by Elizabeth Meriwether Photography
Jarrod Polson

Photo by Kelly Coker
Wes Coker

threw my Ping-Pong paddle at him so hard that it stuck in the drywall behind him, right where his head would have been if he hadn't ducked.

But this book isn't about me. It's about Jarrod. So I mention that because although I taught Jarrod everything I know, I only wish I could say that I taught him everything *he* knows. Somewhere along the way, he learned a lesson that I know I didn't teach him. It took the words of Jesus and me joining the military for me to learn a lesson that, as far as I can tell, Jarrod was born with. It's probably my favorite attribute about him, and if you don't count his blond hair and blue eyes, it's certainly what draws most people to him: he is a team player. He doesn't let his ego get in the way of the team. In a world that tells you to watch your own back and to take care of number one, playing with and watching Jarrod play basketball broke all the rules. He somehow always managed to be the best player on the court without acting like it.

Humility isn't easy to come by. I believe God has gifted Jarrod in this way, and lucky for you, I'm going to let you in on a little secret. Whenever I read books written by two people, I always find myself trying to figure out how much of the book was *actually* written by the famous author. Jarrod and Wes labored over this book together, but there's two ways to know for sure who wrote a particular portion of the book. The first is obvious after what I've just told you about Jarrod: anything that sounds like he is being boastful, or even remotely confident, probably wasn't written by Jarrod. Plain and simple. In order to reveal the second, I will have to tell you a little bit about Wes. Wes is a storyteller. There's a reason that Jarrod wrote the book with Wes instead of me. When Wes tells a story, he *tells* a story. Every aspect is included, the truth is exaggerated if needed, and maybe even a few harmless details are added just for good measure. I think it all stems from the fact that Wes inherited both his and my imagination. I could bore you with plenty of examples, but I'll get to my point. If you find yourself reading about dragon slaying, or maybe even things you've never heard of, that part was probably added in by Wes.

The beauty behind this is that the two of them make a perfect combination. Jarrod finishes a story, and you have to play twenty questions just to get all of the details out of him. Wes finishes reciting a narrative, and you have to ask him twenty questions to figure out which parts actually happened. Fortunately—or unfortunately—I'm the most literal of the bunch. I can honestly say that, as far as my memory serves me, the truth is portrayed throughout the entire text. The stories from our backyard, Southland Christian Church's basketball league, West Jessamine High School, and the University of Kentucky all fit into the life of Jarrod Polson. I am obviously extremely biased, but I think you are in for a real treat. Enjoy!

—Eric Coker

To everyone who feels like an underdog, like their talents aren't good enough to achieve their dreams. All people can live out their dreams, but it may not be the one you imagine. It is far more powerful.

Acknowledgments

I would like to thank a few very special people who have helped me not only with making this book become a reality but who have been instrumental in my life's journey.

My family, immediate and distant, who have always supported me and given me confidence, not only in my basketball career but in all facets of life, thank you.

The Big Blue Nation, the best fan base in America. Thanks for accepting me the way you did during my career at the University of Kentucky. I am forever grateful.

To all of my coaches, thanks for giving me confidence, allowing me to be a part of many successful teams, and pushing me into the man I am today.

To Coach Cal, thanks for giving me the opportunity to play for the University of Kentucky (UK) for four years, but more importantly for showing me how to use a platform to help others.

Christian Student Fellowship, thank you for investing so much time and energy into bringing the gospel to UK students like me.

To all of the friends I've made throughout my twenty-three years—you know who you are. I could write another entire book about the experiences I've had with all of you, so thank you for shaping me into the person I am today.

Dan Lewis, who helped come up with the title of this book, thanks for investing so much of your time into young adults like me, and for helping me get excited and refreshed about what God has planned for the future.

Gregg Lewis and Angela Correll, who graciously gave me helpful advice on how to write, publish, and create my story, thank you.

Max Appel, our team chaplain—our team Bible studies are some of my favorite memories from UK. You had a bigger impact on our team and me individually than you know.

Foreword

During my nearly twenty-three years as a head coach in college basketball, very rarely have I taken a walk-on and put him on scholarship during his entire time in school. It's not that I don't want to—because keep in mind, I was born on the other side of the tracks and had to scratch and claw for everything I got—but you have to be both a great kid who really adds value to the team, as well as being able to help the team in a pinch to go from a walk-on to a scholarship player.

Jarrod Polson epitomized what it meant to be a great teammate, and is why I decided to put him on scholarship. Jarrod's journey as a Kentucky kid who accepted a walk-on spot, quickly worked his way up to becoming a scholarship player, and later developed into a player who won us games, is special.

Now, for me to continue to scholarship a player, he has to show unbelievable growth, not only as a player, but also as a person, and he must continue to add value to the team. Jarrod did all of this, and he did so with a great heart.

During his four years at Kentucky, not only was Jarrod a great teammate, he added value to our team in some really tough situations. The obvious moment that comes to my mind is the game in Brooklyn during our 2012–13 season opener. Jarrod played sparingly the season before during our national championship run, but he prepared like a starter and was ready for his opportunity.

When the time came and his team needed him, Jarrod not only played, he played well and helped us win that game. I can't begin to tell you how proud I was of him. That moment signified to me who Jarrod was as a person and as a member of our team. He always worked hard and was always ready for his opportunity.

I do have one regret with Jarrod. As I look back, having Jarrod change his jersey number prior to his senior year, I can honestly say I fumbled that. As a staff, we got together and talked about it, and no one thought that Jarrod would have a problem with it because he is such a great kid and was so appreciative of having a scholarship the entire time he was at Kentucky. I left it up to the staff to talk to him, and I should have done that myself. I should have had a better feel for the entire situation. I wish I had handled that differently, but Jarrod handled it with class.

On the whole, when I look at Jarrod's time here at Kentucky, I'm not sure there's been any player I have coached who has gotten more out of being in this program than Jarrod. His growth and development as a basketball player and as a person was fun to watch as a coach. He has taken advantage of every opportunity while being here as a player, and nobody walked away with more and appreciated the opportunity more than Jarrod. My hope is that when you read this book, you walk away with that same feeling.

—John Calipari

Contents

— 1 —————————

Jarrod Who?

I'm a pressure shooter; let's see if you are.
    —George Polson (Dad)

"Jarrod!" Calipari yelled across the chasm that separated the Division 1 recruits and the walk-ons.

"Jarrod!" The gazes in my direction confirmed that the other coaches were indeed saying my name while waving emphatically toward the scorer's table. There, at half-court, the tired eyes of analysts consistently shifted back and forth between their laptops and the heated action between the Kentucky Wildcats and Maryland Terrapins. I stared up at the scoreboard, approximately the size of my hometown, and the giant red numbers glared back down at me: sixteen minutes and fifteen seconds.

We weren't even four minutes into the season opener—the year after winning the national tournament with Anthony Davis—and the score was seven to seven. Surely he was meaning to say some other name besides *Jarrod*.

"Jarrod!"

The reality was sinking in, each millisecond noticeably ticking by as my mind slowly accepted that he was not calling for Brandon Knight, Marquis Teague, or John Wall. My contemporaries of yesterday were now on NBA rosters. The unimaginable was happening: Coach was calling on me. I sprinted at light speed, but it felt like slow motion, to midcourt and stared out onto the hardwood. Maryland head coach Mark Turgeon stared at me with a puzzled look and then turned back to his assistant coaches.

"Who's that?"

A fair question. At this point in time, during my out-of-body experience, I'm not sure I knew who I was. I thought I did. After playing for two years at Kentucky with the likes of Michael Kidd-Gilchrist, Terrence Jones, and Doron Lamb, I was completely adjusted to my identity as a victory cigar. I joined the game when the score was lopsided enough to guarantee a Wildcat victory. Despite a mild internal nagging that I had more to offer, I had come to be content with this role. Thankful, even.

"Jarrod?" There are seven people in my family. They know me. My high school barely broke one thousand students. I'm confident that they could identify me. I come from a town of 6,084, and I'm pretty sure most of them know my name. And here I was in Barclay's Center, which holds 18,003 fans, in the lowly city of New York, which has 8.4 million people, during a game being broadcasted by ESPN to millions of viewers all over the country.

"Who's that?" was a very valid question indeed.

Besides the shock, there were nerves. This arena was insane—a lot more like an NCAA tournament game than a season opener. Maryland fans outnumbered the folks dressed in blue, and their bright red fanfare symbolized their desire for blood. After all, it was a fight for bragging rights on various levels—not only aspiring to conquer the previous national champs but also a preseason rank of third in the nation thanks to a Calipari-infused reload with Alex

Poythress, Archie Goodwin, and Nerlens Noel. This place was loud. And the pressure was immense. Honestly, I didn't know if I was ready for it. The only thing I can compare my nerves to was what I experienced vicariously through Maximus Meridius in the movie *Gladiator* when he looks out of the tunnel into the arena knowing he is about to go fight for his life on that battlefield. I know that seems like quite the hyperbole, but as I watched these athletic, Division 1 phenoms battling it out on the hardwood, I could hardly believe that I was about to enter the war.

———

The most significant dead ball of my life ripped me into the action, whether I was ready or not. "I got you," I said to Ryan Harrow, our hands colliding as I felt the weight of this cosmic torch he handed me. Clearly, Ryan had not recovered fully from his bout with the flu the previous week, and his play showed it. And now all the pressure was handed off to me.

I should have been a nervous wreck, limbs shaking and perspiring uncontrollably, but as I stepped onto that court, an overwhelming peace swept over me. Suddenly, the pressure seemed to evaporate, and the circumstances began to fade away. I was playing the game I loved. The fear dissipated, and the reckless spirit I had been so out of touch with the last two years was returning. I knew somehow that everything was under control. The soft voice inside was back. And I desperately needed to tune out the other voices if this was going to end well for me. The smack talk of Maryland and Turgeon questioning who I was did not do much for my confidence. If I could have heard what the commentators were adding, I wouldn't have found any solace there either. Dick Vitale gave his honest and bleak prediction for my time on the court: "He's a player who works really hard in practice, but here he just needs to give guys some rest and not turn the ball over."

The score was Kentucky with twelve to Maryland's nine. It was clearly anyone's game. Willie Cauley Stein had the ball in the post, and defenders swarmed. I was at the top of the key and noticed the lane parting like the red sea. Instinct took over, and I darted through the free throw line right as Willie noticed my dash, leading me with a perfect pass. I caught the ball in the paint, squeezed through two defenders who seemed surprised to see me, and then elevated toward the backboard to drop in a right-handed layup off the glass. My first two points of the season (surpassing the one point I had the entire previous year) were not of the inconsequential, victory cigar type. They were of the "you didn't see me coming, but now we're up five" variety.

In my house in Wilmore, my mom and dad started popping Lipitor to offset the pending heart attacks. In Indiana, my older brother nearly dropped a wine glass while working at a restaurant. In South Carolina, my other brother nearly jumped through the ceiling. My friends back at Christian Student Fellowship exploded with screams of excitement. And the coaches wearing red were still asking, "Jarrod who?"

Several possessions later, I had another chance to develop my résumé when Archie Goodwin's jump shot came off the rim hard, deflecting the ball out of the paint. It came right into my hands at the free throw line. My first thought was to bring it back out and set up the offense, but by this point I felt confident enough to take the shot. Nothing but net. My stats at this point allowed no reason for me to be taken out of the game—I was two for two from the field, had two assists, and had zero turnovers. When I came in, we had been neck and neck, and now Kentucky was up twenty-three to nineteen. The magic was building, so I stayed in the game until the first half ended. I had no miraculous offensive feats, but I played solid defense and ran the offense well enough that we went into the locker room with a comfortable lead, up forty-nine to thirty-six.

During halftime, I didn't know what to expect moving into the next act. I was excited about my performance but knew that didn't guarantee any playing time during the rest of the game. So there was no surprise whatsoever when the game resumed and I found myself in my normal spot: on the bench. As I sat, I had a front-row seat while I watched our comfortable lead slowly slip away.

It didn't take long for Maryland to make a run of their own. They came out of the gate outscoring us fifteen to zero, tying the game at fifty-three. With eight minutes left in regulation, Coach Cal had seen enough, and his glance returned down the chasm as our eyes locked.

"Polson!" he yelled, nodding again toward the scorer's table.

I smiled, and the saga continued, this time with even more magic than the first.

First, there was the technological mystery. The Barclay Center was new, and so some kinks still needed to be worked out. But whatever the cause, a certain malfunction occurred on the main scoreboard while I was in the game. The team lineup screen experienced some inexplicable error so that the P of my last name, "Polson," was missing. Over half of the fans present in the stadium that night didn't know who I was, and millions of people watching at home didn't know who I was, and even Maryland's coach didn't know who I was. And to add insult to injury, neither did the scoreboard. In place of the P in my name, something showed up to fill the space. It appeared to be some kind of dagger symbol. This could have been some technological faux pas, but perhaps the mysterious scoreboard knew something no one else did.

Time in this game was winding down, and it was clear that neither team was going to run away with an outrageous lead. The game was going to be won by whoever showed the most grit, or as the old coaching cliché says ... whoever wanted it more. That inner desire is not revealed as much by points scored as it is by a tenacious hunger for rebounds or loose balls.

Now, I was not a player known for my offensive rebounding prowess. In all honesty, I wasn't a player known for anything besides the iconic "White Boy Academy" YouTube videos with Kyle Wiltjer. But with five minutes left, I watched as Nerlens Noel made an aggressive post move. I had a feeling that he might miss the hook shot, so I sped into the lane as the ball rimmed off right into my hands for an easy tip in to put us back into the lead by one point. Then a few minutes later the most improbable play of the game and potentially my career was about to unfold.

We were up by two points, and Nerlens was at the line for a free throw. Coach Cal deserves the credit for this play because I vividly remember him barking out these instructions: "When the ball hits the rim, rush into the lane and get it."

I had a flashback to my old days playing church ball. When commands are given, there is no room for failure—they simply must be carried out, regardless of the difficulty or seeming impossibility of the task. In this instance, the idea seemed asinine because I was the guy standing outside of the three-point line to protect our basket on the defensive end. Regardless, I obeyed Coach's command, and as soon as it ricocheted off the rim, I sprinted into the lane. It was a valiant effort, but Maryland's Pe'Shon Howard grabbed the rebound before I could get there.

However, as he pivoted, I snuck my hand through his arms and somehow jarred the ball loose without fouling him, winding up with the stolen treasure just outside of our paint. Maryland barely had time to realize I had the ball before my instinct to get to the rim had taken over. I took one dribble into the paint and jump stopped as I squared up against James Padgett, their six-foot, eight-inch, 225-pound center. If I was going to score on him, it wasn't going to be a dunk. It would need to be an acrobatic miracle.

Blast-off. As I jumped toward the goal, I pump faked to the right side of the rim, brought the ball way back down with my left hand, and released a lurching left-handed prayer that kissed the glass at the highest place possible. I fell to the ground, looking up at the ball as it suspended on the front of the rim. Time stood still, our wide-eyed bench all holding onto their chairs, knees bending lower and lower as they willed the ball into the goal. Something broke through, whether telekinesis or my family's prayers, and the ball splashed down through the nets about the same time I scrambled back up to my feet. At least, that's what I think happened.

Luke Winn, writer for *Sports Illustrated*, was able to give a more professional analysis of the play, exposing the exact science behind what I had pulled off: "Polson then converted an absurd, spinning, pumping layup around the Terps' trees, putting UK up 67-63 with 3:44 left."

———

The bench celebration may have been more exciting than the entire crowd's reaction combined. The walk-on clan jumped up and down uncontrollably, mouths wide open with screams of ecstasy, beating their chests like Tarzan, creeping out onto the floor as though Kentucky had just won another championship. Kyle Wiltjer jumped up and down and pumped his fists like he had just won the lottery.

But the game wasn't over.

The score was seventy to sixty-nine, with seven seconds left, and Kyle was throwing the ball into play. None of my teammates were open, so I cut right toward Kyle and received the pass, only to get fouled instantly. This was the moment I had been waiting for my entire life. I had a chance to go to the line and sink two free throws to secure a victory for the University of Kentucky. This was truly a once-in-a-lifetime experience, completely unchartered territory as a player on this team. At the same time, I had been there thousands of times before. I had fantasized and acted out a situation like this in more imaginative scenarios than I could count. But now I was in front of eighteen thousand fans and millions of television viewers and actually had the real-life responsibility of leading the Wildcats to their first win of the year. No pressure.

As I got to the line, the nerves began to overwhelm me like a wildfire. My legs began to physically shake, and my hands began to sweat. But as the nerves increased, so did the recognition of the holy presence inside my heart as I prayed and took a deep breath. Closing my eyes, suddenly I was somewhere else—not in New York City anymore. I was back in Wilmore, Kentucky, and my little five-year-old arms took a couple of dribbles to pause before my free throw. I looked up at the slightly bent rim on my worn-down basketball hoop and felt the breeze on my face telling me to wait one more moment so the wind didn't throw off this monumental moment. My mom was inside making dinner, a celebratory feast I could only partake in if I led my beloved Wildcats to victory. My eyes refocused behind the lenses of my glasses. Our white picket fence blurred in the background as the rim came once again into focus.

Suddenly the trees blowing in the wind became a mass of wildly waving arms, and the rustling leaves became the oceanic roar of the crowd. My five-year-old surroundings were gone. But the peace was still there. I was ready.

I took one dribble and let it go. My release felt so awkward that I thought my shot was going to be off right. It sailed in slow motion toward the rim, proving that it had no plans to fail me. *Swish*!

Now we were up sixty-nine to seventy-one, so another free throw with only seven seconds left would force them to hit a rushed three-point shot. A quick prayer, deep breath, dribble, and a shot. This time as I released it, I thought I left it short, but again, the ball had other plans. Another swish!

With that shot, the victory was looming. Maryland dribbled down the court and took a leaning, hopeless shot contested by the person you wouldn't have wanted in the defensive vicinity: Noel. The shot bounced off the right side of the backboard, with no whistle to give the Terrapins any hope. The euphoria began. The stands roared in celebration of our victory, the sound of pure joy ringing in my ears. And for those watching on TV, their ears were filled with the familiar unbridled enthusiasm of Dick Vitale.

"He's a kid that we didn't anticipate playing a lot at all tonight. I talked to the coaching staff, and they gave players... they never gave me this kid. Tell you one thing... he is earning some PT tonight! Kentucky survives, and they ought to thank and hug Mr. Polson. An unknown player has been the star of the moment for the Cats here tonight. Made a couple of big free throws, had a great offensive rebound, didn't turn the ball over. Played quality minutes. Big time performance for a kid they didn't count on."

I was a nobody in the grand scheme of college basketball before entering the Barclay's Arena. And when I left, I was trending on Twitter. "Who's that?" would no longer be a valid question. The walk-on label would be replaced with the respect of a valuable, high-stakes player. However, my story doesn't begin here, and it doesn't end here either. Truth be told, my college years still had more moments when I was used as a victory cigar than as a player absorbing the glory from a hard-fought victory. But I'll never forget how good it felt to be a dagger.

— 2 —

I Had an Impossible Dream

To accomplish great things, we must not only act,
but also dream; not only plan, but also believe.
—*Anatole France*

My journey to the University of Kentucky began with a dream. You ask any elementary classroom in the nation to tell their dreams, and you'll get about as many answers as there are kids: firefighter, policeman, chef, teacher, veterinarian, pilot, doctor, astronaut, actor, professional video game tester. The list will grow as each young visionary verbalizes his or her creative, outlandish, and extremely unlikely hopes for the future. And the honest teacher will gently persuade Jimmy and Steven to rethink their goals of making money with space travel or by playing Madden because they probably don't have what it takes.

In Kentucky, this is not the case for those who bleed blue. In the bluegrass state, teachers don't need every student to speak up. They simply ask from the front of the class, "Who wants to play basketball for Kentucky?" And without looking around, all the students launch their hands into the air with the zeal of a soldier ready to march on the front lines. And no one is discouraged from volunteering his or her hand. There is no soapbox sermon about how everyone can't be an athlete, because then no one would be left to sell pretzels at the games. No statement is made about the difficulty or slim chances of the dream coming true because the very desire for this calling is holy and must be encouraged. And secretly, no matter what age, it's still the teacher's dream too.

This is the way things are in Wilmore, Kentucky, where I grew up. Like all great Kentucky dads, mine taught our family the importance of two priorities: church on Sunday morning and watching every UK basketball game. He grew up in Harlan County, mountain territory, but moved to Lexington after college and met my mom. It could have been that he didn't see coal mining in his future and that greater occupational potential was waiting in the big city. But I know the truth: Rupp Arena, our state's Mecca, was tugging at his heart. So my four siblings and I grew up in a small town with an awesome family, and I was the middle child. My two older brothers seemed like grown men since four years separated me from Eric and another four from him and Wes. Ashley, Alyse, and I were much closer in age, all born within a span of four years. Needless to say, our house was a hive of activity, and a large part of that involved sports.

I don't remember when I first watched a Kentucky basketball game because I would have been in utero. Maybe that's why one of the first gross motor accomplishments I achieved as a toddler was not walking. Legend has it that before I could take any steps, I was able to shoot a basketball into the Little Tikes goal that took a prominent place in our living room. By age five, I could rattle off the name and number of every single player on Kentucky's roster. I made up songs about Ron Mercer and Anthony Epps. I would strategically wait in the driveway twenty minutes before my dad would come home so I could trap him into playing a game. Even though my brothers were significantly older and larger than me, we would still play, and they would crush me. It was equivalent to growing up in a Spartan village where everything in my childhood was designed to train and make me stronger for the battlefield of basketball. Okay, not entirely, but you get the point. Basketball seemed not only to be a religion where I grew up, but it was also in my genes. This was a loyal lineage passed down from my father's father and probably his father before that. There was a reason my papaw affectionately called me his "lil' wildcat."

Fully accepting the prophetic circumstances of my youth, I played basketball as often as I got the chance. If I couldn't convince my siblings to play games against me, I would resort to playing them in my imagination. I would spend hours in the basement, creating tournaments and playing them all the way through. For as much creative energy I put into forming these brackets, the championship game always had the same ending: Kentucky winning (usually against Duke) with a three-point buzzer beater. And if I missed the shot, a foul was undoubtedly called, and I would sink the free throws to make sure the Wildcats prevailed. If I missed the free throws, then obviously an opposing player had stepped across the line before my shot was released. It was incredible how consistently those imaginary amateurs would make that mistake, but only on my missed attempts.

———

Dreams are like drugs for kids. I put all my energy, heart, and soul into my vision and was absolutely consumed by the desire to make it happen. But even as an elementary school kid, I could feel the weight of difficulty in making it come true. College athletes seemed like gods from another world sent here for our worship and admiration. I remember getting autographs from players like Kenny "SkyWalker," marveling at his size and skill, as if he were truly a magical being. Joining their ranks seemed impossible since I was clearly just a normal human, born of an earthly woman, with no miraculous conception story or unique marks of divine intervention. Not only was I lacking a positive sign that my life was marked for the chosen priesthood of ballers, but there were also a couple of physical barriers that seemed to point in the complete opposite direction of college athlete. For starters, my skin was this awful white color. That didn't seem to match the prerequisite skin tone that I noticed in the great players I looked up to. But I assumed that could change with enough time; there were still plenty of years until college.

The other issue seemed even more problematic: my eyes. I was born just shy of being legally blind. This would have been okay at first since there are two kinds of glasses in the world. The first kind is the pair of glasses that makes someone look sophisticated and edgy—maybe even sexy. They're the kind of glasses that, when worn by the appropriate NBA player, would make everyone go out and buy a pair—even people with twenty/twenty vision. And then, there's the other kind. The second pair is the type that has obnoxiously huge circle frames that are in no way fashionable and lenses so large that you need special ear hooks to make sure they stay on your face. This is important because if they fall off and break, your life is over. You're so blind without glasses that every light bulb looks like a firework and you can't recognize a familiar face three feet in front of you. If you're lucky they will fall and land on your foot, which is good because the lenses won't break; however, it's also bad because your foot will surely smash like a pumpkin.

I had this second pair of glasses. And as you can imagine, they were not the proper eyewear for an aspiring UK basketball player;

they were the proper eyewear for those aiming at careers writing novels about space travel or playing video games professionally.

Now, maybe this wouldn't have been such a bad thing if my extracurricular choices during my early school years weren't equally destructive for my image as a future Wildcat. My mother is extremely musical and very well could have had herself a career down in Nashville if she hadn't thought raising a family was infinitely more important. She bestowed me with some of that musical gene, and I picked up piano the year before I went to elementary school. I really liked playing, even though I knew I couldn't let it get in the way of my first love. But music is easier to get involved in than athletics when you're in fourth grade, so since I couldn't play on a school basketball team, I played the role of Bob Cratchit in *A Christmas Carol*. At that age I could nail the part of soprano with ease. I am fairly confident that I cracked someone's glasses singing the highest note in the line, "Sometimes I ask *myself*, is there more to happiness?"

But my glasses were fine. They were way too thick.

Those two elements were definitely not in my favor. Plus, besides the obvious physical barriers to my dream was the realism of my mother. The teachers wouldn't snuff out a dream to play basketball at UK, and my dad certainly wasn't going to do the job. My dad always taught us that whatever we could dream, we could do. My mom's philosophy was far more grounded, as she eloquently reminded my brothers and me by saying things like this: "Playing basketball at Kentucky? That's impossible. One out of a million people in the nation will be a UK basketball player."

She wasn't trying to be a party pooper; she just wanted to spare us depression in the event that such an ambitious goal wouldn't be reached. Even though I was young, naïve, and ambitious, something about my mom's words seemed true. I could find hope in a player like Steve Masiello, who was a six-foot-one white kid who weighed 170 pounds but still found himself on Kentucky's roster as a walk-on. Yet even his story, when understood within the context of the demigod college athletes, kind of takes the wind out of a young dreamer's sails. Masiello was an absolute high school phenomenon: in his senior year at Harvey in Katonah, New York, he averaged 34.5 points *and* 8 assists per game. As a Wildcat, Masiello barely saw the floor. His senior year at Kentucky, he scored one point. The whole season.

Maybe my mom was right. If only one in a million can make the team, it didn't seem like the buck-toothed, blind thespian had good odds. And even if I did make the team, which was next to impossible, actually playing a significant role and getting off the bench seemed like a double miracle.

I could have put it all behind me then and quit wishing on a star. After all, I had my music to fall back on. There were other dreams I could have run with that would have been a lot more likely for a little nerd from Wilmore, Kentucky. But as I grew up, I couldn't put the ball down. I loved the sport too much, and I felt alive when I played. Plus, it seemed like all of the people I heard about in this Bible my parents read to me had even more ridiculous dreams. These characters seemed to have this rock-solid faith that regardless of how impossible something seemed, there was another force at work behind the scenes that could take human risk and turn it into something unbelievable. All they knew was that they had to be obedient to what they could do and make the simple choices they could make. So I didn't put the ball down, and I kept believing in the dream. After all, it couldn't hurt to try.

— 3 ———————

Confidence of Family

You are never too old to set another
goal or to dream a new dream.
—C. S. Lewis

Here's the thing about dreams. They are really fun to think about and to stay up late at night and talk about. But they are really scary to pursue, if they are dreams worth chasing. It's one thing to fantasize about slaying a dragon and a whole different thing altogether to pick up a sword on Saturday morning to go hunting for one. At home on my Little Tikes goal I was a prodigy, not to mention undefeated in the tournaments I played in my imagination. But as I grew up, it was time for the tests of a bigger stage. If Horace Grant could play alongside Michael Jordan wearing those mammoth goggles, then surely my church's youth basketball league could suffer the debut of me and my obnoxious glasses.

Perhaps you've never had the pleasure of watching elementary-aged basketball, so allow me to sum it up for you. At this level, there is really no reason to have referees. There are no traveling violations because only a few players can actually dribble. But that doesn't matter, because dribbling is unnecessary since most players just shoot the ball from wherever they happen to find it. I had a player on my team who would literally launch up a shot right where he got the rebound—a defensive rebound. Despite being a little overzealous, this showed that he was actually ahead of the curve, because although his full-court Hail Mary had no prayer of going in, it did show he knew which goal he was supposed to shoot on. For most players, being aware of such minor details like which hoop belonged to them was a level of understanding they would aspire to in middle school.

There were a couple players in the league who were different. A select few had big brothers, were a little older than the others, or had the basketball gene in their blood, or they had some other advantage that put them into the advanced minority. And I was in that group. At that level I could dribble through my legs and behind my back and drive the lane with my head up. But most dangerously, I understood how to pass. And when I say dangerous, I don't mean for the opposing team but my fellow teammates. The shoot-first mentality meant they were never looking to make a pass or to receive one. As a result most of my possible assists resulted in balls to the face or passes out of bounds because our players weren't watching.

Needless to say, our team didn't always win the championship. But it was the first time that I was able to showcase my talent at a young age. One of the most entertaining family videos captured a theme in my basketball personality that revolved around my reluctance to take charge. If I had chosen to control more of those early games, I am sure they could've had different outcomes. But my brother Eric caught one of those moments on film that showcased my hidden potential.

We were down by about fifteen points with a couple minutes left. A comeback was impossible, but Eric was fed up with my complacency and started yelling coaching instructions to me from the bleachers. "Steal it, Jarrod!" he yelled as they threw the ball in from under our goal. Upon my brother's request, I initiated the first ever one-man full-court press. I ran up to their guard, forced him to pick up his dribble, and stripped the ball away without fouling him. (At least the ref didn't blow his whistle … They generally reserved that for when players tackled each other during a shot.) I could have just banked in a little gimme in the paint, but I heard Coach Eric again from the stands: "Shoot a three!"

The other team was doubly confused. First, they had never seen a full-court press or that kind of defensive intensity with about a minute left to play. Second, they had never seen a player go backward to take a *longer* shot than the one that offered itself. I took a couple dribbles to get behind the three-point line and thrust it up toward the rim with both hands. Swish. My family went crazy. The stands went nuts, even though at this point it was far too little too late. What mattered was that they had just witnessed the first three-pointer the league had ever seen. And my brother Eric—well, let's just say he was the most enthusiastic of the fans.

"Steal it again, Jarrod!"

There was another inbound pass, followed by another confused point guard under pressure, another foul-less strip, and for the second time in three seconds, I had the ball again.

"Shoot a three!" Eric trumpeted again from the stands.

I dribbled back behind the line and heaved up another bomb. Boom. The second one rained down another triple on the scoreboard. At this point the crowd was really on their feet, curious if this circus-like magic show could continue.

"Jarrod, steal it again!"

By this point the play was fairly well rehearsed. The poor point guard knew I was coming, but he wasn't one of the chosen few who understood what a pass was. So for the third time in a row, I stole the ball like candy from a baby.

"Yes!" Eric yelled, at this point so excited for me that he was practically on the court, in awe that his instructions had such a tangible effect on my game. "Shoot it again!" I dialed up long distance once more and connected for a hat trick of three pointers … all within about a minute.

We didn't win the game, but we did come within a handful of points to dragging the opposing team into overtime. And my family had one of the most comical highlight reels ever before captured on film. The kind of unbelievable spectacle you would pay money to see when the Harlem Globetrotters came into town was on display for free in an obscure gymnasium at Southland Christian Church.

In the movies, after the buzzer went off, scouts from UK would have come out of the stands to offer me a full scholarship as a Wildcat. And I would have agreed, under the condition that my brother Eric was also signed on as head coach. But this was not the case. The mini-miracle that day didn't mean much to anyone outside the building. And to me the whole thing didn't feel like a great showcase of talent so much as it was a testimony to the power of submission to an older sibling's orders. I was just doing what he told me to do. What's incredible to me is that my actual performance had little effect on my belief in myself. What mattered was that *someone else* believed in me. I never would have attempted those steals or those ridiculous threes if my older brother hadn't been yelling instructions from the bleachers.

This lack of self-confidence followed me into school basketball, despite all the natural ability I had. My older brothers weren't free to micromanage my defensive choices and shot selection, since our careers never crossed paths while I was in middle school. By the time I got into sixth grade, Wes was in college and Eric was in his sophomore year of high school. There was one time I remember getting to play with Eric as a teammate and not a coach. I was in eighth grade, so by this time he was playing at the varsity level as a senior. But they let me dress for a few games, and on one occasion we got to run the floor together. In middle school my game revolved around driving to the basket. Getting rid of the glasses in exchange for contacts was like a life-changing conversion for me and my versatility. It's a worrisome enterprise to consistently drive the lane while worrying if your glasses are going to fall off right before you shoot. And yet, those glasses made me look better on paper because they added about twenty pounds to my listed weight. At a varsity level, it was fairly difficult to compete for a kid who was five feet, two inches and weighed in at one hundred pounds. Still, I'll never forget getting into the game and attacking that rim in hopes of being underestimated. I kissed my layup off the glass but a little too hard. Luckily, Eric was there for the tip-in. So during the only game we got to play together, he was there to clean up my trash. But a day was coming when there would be no older brother to have my back as a teammate ... or as a coach.

— 4 —

Confidence of a Coach

A player who makes a team great is much
more valuable than a great player.
—*John Wooden*

My sophomore year is when I really started getting some playing time at the varsity level. But it was pretty intimidating on a number of levels. There was a reason I quit playing football as I entered the high school years; I came in as a freshman at five foot five and 120 pounds. There were thoughts of being a hitting dummy during practice for the seniors every day that I didn't particularly enjoy. Of course, basketball was no picnic either, especially when your forte is driving into traffic to create your shots. My body seemed several years away from even thinking about hitting puberty, which always brings about its own set of mental side effects. Combined with that was the psychological issues brought about through borrowing playing time from a group of talented seniors who were not too keen on the idea of having the limelight shared with a scrawny sophomore. I wanted to do well, and I would have liked to score more, but I also wanted to do everything I could to keep the upperclassmen happy. Everything about playing at that level with my size and experience was intimidating. The nerves got to me so much that during the very first game I ever played as a sophomore, my first stat in the books was a technical foul. I was so anxious to get into the game that I left too early from the scorer's table. Oops.

I had a breakout game when I scored twenty-seven points around Christmastime, but it was like every point I scored had to be squeezed and prodded out of me by Coach Hammonds because of my fear of my teammates' disapproval. And while playing that way kept me in good graces with the seniors, my refusal to lead like I could have hurt our chances in the long run. We made it to the regional championship and were one win away from going to Rupp Arena for a shot at winning state. That loss brought a disappointment I had never felt before and gave the underclassmen and me a fire in our guts the next two years. My team needed my talent. But even more, they needed my leadership. When I created my own shots, defenses had to compensate. When they collapsed in on me, the assist factory could begin operation. And when I began to grasp the power of my role on the team as a point guard, the magic could really begin.

For me, that magic became a reality during my junior year. My family believed in me. My teammates believed in me. But I was still trying to decide if I believed in me. Growing up in Wilmore, Kentucky, and going to West Jessamine High School, it was easy to feel like a bit of a big fish. And yet if I was honest with myself, I knew I lived in a small pond. In our schedule, we didn't face a ton of powerhouse teams, so getting any kind of exposure in my neck of the woods took a major accomplishment. For me, there was no better time to have that kind of performance than when we played a team like Lexington Catholic. Just down the road from us was a monster of a team, ranked number eight in the state of Kentucky, who loved coming into our house with their D-1 prospects and wiping the floor with us country hicks. Our school always seemed to get hyped about this game even though they weren't our main rival. We reserved the harshest hatred for East Jessamine, who any of us would have gladly laid down our lives in battle to conquer. They were our true nemesis, our Darth Vader, our Sauron, and our Voldemort all wrapped into one. To beat them was probably more significant than winning a state championship, and that's just how it was growing up in Jessamine County. But still, when the Knights of Lexington Catholic rode into town, it was always a momentous occasion. A victory against a team like theirs was extremely unlikely, but on the rare occasions when we could get the best of them, it would infuse in our season a spark of hope that we might be able to live out some variation of *Hoosiers* and make a run at a state title.

If there was a turning point in our season, and in my career as a basketball player, this night was the golden opportunity. I don't imagine that Catholic's scouting report of our team flagged any names of players that they needed to worry about. But we were very aware of at least one of the dangers in their ranks: Vee Sanford. If that name rings a bell now, it's because Vee ended up as a guard for the Dayton Flyers, a Cinderella team in the 2014 NCAA tournament who made it to the elite eight after knocking off Ohio State and Syracuse along the way. Needless to say, in high school Vee Sanford was among the most elite athletes we'd have the chance to play against.

If you were a betting man, you'd be safe to assume that a wager in favor of West Jessamine would be about as silly as a wager that the Cubs would win the World Series. Or if you're more familiar with David and Goliath, it was a bit like that story. Only, David had it easy. His fight was less than a minute, and he only needed to pull off one lucky shot. We needed to pull off about fifty lucky shots to rack up over a hundred points over a span of thirty-two minutes if we would have any hope to slay this giant.

But as fate would have it, the miracle was in our favor that night. We amassed enough points to conquer our foe with a final score of 102 to 92. Of those 102 points, I was able to claim 51 of them. But even as crazy as a 51-point game seemed, I didn't mean to score that much. In fact, they forced me to. Thirty of them came from the free throw line. They must have brought up every sub all the way down to their middle school rosters to keep their press running at a level where they could foul as much as they did. They lost that game because their press wasn't working but they never fixed it, and I just kept exploiting it, breaking a state record for free throws attempted and made along the way. After the game Vee Sanford was quoted as saying,

"Jarrod Polson is the best point guard I've ever played against."

And with that game brought about a change of trajectory for our season and my path as a player. My name started to get out. No longer did I have the luxury of being an unknown and unscouted player going into games. But the more people focused on me, the better I did. Over thirty-point games began to be commonplace. And when I didn't score like crazy, because of the amount of adjustments made by our opponent's defensive strategies, it allowed me to play like a true point guard by opening up the floodgates of scoring for everyone else. My playing to the best of my ability made everyone else play better, and as a team we were really starting to see the reality of a state-tournament run.

My junior year we climbed all the way to the final four, and senior year to the elite eight, when we lost to another *Hoosier*-esque team: Shelby Valley. Though we never tasted the state championship victory, both years' runs were historic events for our school and incredible to witness for our community. Commentators made jokes during the sweet sixteen at Rupp Arena about the town our school was in: "Now is the time to steal whatever you want in Nicholasville because it's very likely that every person in the city is in downtown Lexington today to root for West Jessamine."

The amount of momentum that basketball dreams can build in the lives of players, families, schools, and communities is truly a remarkable thing. It wasn't that many years ago that I was a kid in diapers singing songs about Cameron Mills, performing in musicals with my humongous glasses, and hoping that one day I would get my shot at playing basketball on a big stage. And here I was, seventeen years old, playing at Rupp Arena with my high school buddies and building a résumé for myself that had all the markings of a Division 1 basketball stud. You would think that this all would've gone to my head—that arrogance would have crept in and replaced humility with egotism and my faith with pride. Yet for all my success, my head didn't seem to be growing too big for my neck. Maybe it was that my neck was so strong after carrying those glasses for so many years, but I think it was something deeper.

— 5 ————————

The End of a Dream

Failure is good. It's fertilizer.
—*Rick Pitino*

The word *self-confidence* is a bit ironic. It may be the gauge of how confident you feel about yourself, but that gauge is hopelessly dependent on what *others* feel about your potential. At least that's true for me. We are what we think others think we are. So if that's the case, at this point in my story I should've been spiking in my self-confidence. As I said, my family believed in me. My team believed in me. Even Vee Sanford believed in me. Yet in the face of all that support and rock-solid optimism, I still managed to have this conversation with my coach, Damon Kelley. We were sitting in his office in the back of the school, just the two of us, and after some small talk, I quickly got to the point.

"I guess I'll just play at a small school or go to UK and study engineering but not play basketball."

"Not play basketball? What do you mean not play basketball?" Damon asked, shocked at my passive comment.

That was a good question. What did I mean? How could I say that? My childhood dream for as long as I could remember was not just a fairy tale anymore … it was reaching out to me, and I just needed to extend my hand. But that was scary. And it was easier to change my desire than it was to pick up the sword and go after the dragon.

"Listen, Jarrod. You're *way too good* to just stop playing."

Coach Kelley was always pushing me. Different people in my journey helped mold me in unique ways. I didn't have the confidence to be a scorer. Coach Hammonds helped me break that fear. I didn't think I was good enough to play Division 1 ball. Coach Kelley helped me believe in my talent, and I will always be thankful for that. If there is a recipe for making dreams come true, talent is definitely a major ingredient. But at least equally important is our own confidence in the possibility of those dreams, as well as the people in our lives who push us to take the risks involved in making them happen. There are so many talented people in the world just sitting and waiting for their time to shine, but they allow their fear of failure to be greater than the gift they have to share with the world. I was about to allow all my desire and God-given talent to hide in the shadows for a college career studying something I didn't even really care about. Why? Because sometimes the choice to take the leap is hindered by the uncertainty we feel about the landing—unless we're pushed.

———

I think all high school juniors and seniors would agree that the college decision is a daunting one. When you're standing on the edge, trying to know where to jump, it's safe to assume that most people ask for a burning bush to alleviate the pressure of such a momentous fork in the road. Then it becomes understandable that parents put babies in onesies with school logos, brainwashing them from birth. It's not parental manipulation or restricting your offspring's freedom. It is a gift to be spared from the agonizingly nightmarish decision of choosing a college for yourself.

And by the end of my senior season, I started to get a little worried about what I would be doing the following year. Despite my D-1 stats and résumé, my physical stature on the roster appeared more suited for a golf caddy scholarship. At a time when most athletes knew where they were going to play, I had a few options that were well beneath my dream as it relates to basketball. My future seemed bound for Division 3 or NAIA schools such as Transylvania, Centre, Asbury, or Cedarville. If my hopes for playing at the highest level were going to be realized, it was going to come down to how far we went in the postseason. And at the start of district tournaments, this pressure really started to sink in. A loss at this point of the year would put the dream to sleep forever. And as fate would have it, our first round we were playing against East Jessamine, our huge in-town rival. We had collected a hat trick of victories against them that year, which meant they were out for revenge, threefold.

Lying in bed the night before that game, I was more nervous than I had ever been for any other game in my life. Sitting up in bed, looking at the red and blue walls of my room, I knew that tomorrow night's game would have a huge impact on the next four years of my life, and that was a feeling that I had never really experienced before. There is the kind of nervous that cripples you and the kind that energizes unprecedented performance. And luckily I was infused with the second kind the next night, paving the way with a triple-double in a game when we conquered our rival by thirty points. So the journey began on a good foot.

The following game was more of a nail-biter: an overtime win against Mercer County that propelled us to the regional tournament. This meant higher competition, higher exposure, but higher stakes.

We went in knowing that it would take three victories in a row to win the tournament and get back to Rupp Arena. When I should have been more anxious than ever, I remember praying to God and feeling an odd peace that our team would be fine and that I would have my chance to shine. Something changed in me during this time that I'm not sure I can fully explain. I only know that the way I felt, played, and spoke was radiating with confidence.

"Last year this team saw a historic run. But if we don't make another run like that this year, it will be a disappointment," Coach Kelley said to me about the team.

I looked him right in the eyes and said, "Don't worry; we're definitely going back to state. I'll make sure of it."

I never said things like that, but this new peace and calmness inside of me was allowing something to take root that I had heard about constantly but never fully been able to grasp. And yet now, at the perfect time, I had started to believe.

I hit a floater at the buzzer to win the first game. I scored forty points in our second game, carrying us to the next. Then I scored thirty-two points to put us back into the state tournament for the second year in a row. Everything was clicking, worry didn't seem to faze me, and I simply loved playing the game. I knew I had to score, so I did. Even my three pointers were falling, which was something that had been off most of the year. It was almost as though I had returned to the Southland leagues as a kid, playing unconsciously as I listened to my older brother speak confidence into my shot. Only now, the voice was coming from the inside.

I've always wondered if God interacts with the physics of our lives or just gives us certain gifts that allow us to do incredible things. Did He personally direct the stone flung from David's sling or simply give him the gift of accuracy? While I don't imagine to have settled that debate, I do know that I have experienced what it is like to do something with a confidence and peace inside that wasn't from me. And the whole time I was thinking that these games were part of a bigger plan than I could comprehend. Time would tell.

———————

The stage had expanded as much as possible for me as we marched through the tournament. And soon we found ourselves going head to head against Elisha Justice (who had committed at this point to Louisville) and his team, Shelby Valley. This was the clash of the Titans as arguably the two top point guards in the state would face off against each other. The state championship trophy is prize enough for any team of high school students, but the word was spreading of an even more coveted prize. Apparently, rumors were circulating that UK was looking for an in state point guard to come on board with the team. And Elisha Justice, who had the makings of Mr. Basketball, only needed to lead his top-rated Wildcats to a state title and all the pieces would fall together for him. He wouldn't even need to change mascots.

Of course, I had different visions of the ending to this story. The underdog card burned more strongly in my heart than ever before, and in my head all I needed to do was lead my team to a win against Justice on Kentucky's legendary Rupp Arena home court. Following the game, Coach Cal would come up to me, shake my hand, and offer me a full-ride scholarship. After the long and crazy ride, only one victory stood between me and all my childhood dreams.

And then came the tears. I didn't ever think it was worthy to cry over sports, but this game crushed me at a much deeper level. The game was out of reach with a minute left, and I was substituted out to watch the last seconds unfold. I took my seat on the bench, desperately trying to hold my tears back, but I couldn't. We put up a valiant fight and played our hearts out on that floor, but it wasn't enough for Shelby Valley. They were an incredible, almost magical team. And I felt devastated that I didn't do enough to lead our team to a state championship. I felt defeated that this game was the last of my high school career and I had just watched my dream of playing for UK slip out of my fingers forever. I had survived masses and made it to the final two out of a million who have a chance to play at Kentucky. My chances were that of a coin toss, and I lost. It was unbelievable to come that far and taste defeat so close to the ultimate goal.

I had never experienced anything like that before. I believed in something so strongly, and everything seemed to be lining up so that it could become a reality, and then everything was taken away by a kid named Elisha Justice, which oozed with biblical weight. It felt so unjust. After all I had been through, it didn't seem like this was the scene before the ending credits would roll. But I suppose this is what life is meant to do to teenagers. It puffs them up with self-confidence and hope and crazy dreams so maybe there's some chance of survival when they get dashed upon the rocks of reality.

It just seemed so disproportionate. There had been so much belief, so much energy, so much passion, so much preparation, so much time, so much family support, so much watching film, so much worry about getting the right exposure, so much conditioning, so much dreaming, so much doubting, so much doubt smashing, so much re-dreaming, and so much hype. Then we lost. And it was all over with so little to show for any of it. There was so little trophy, so little hope of playing basketball anywhere that got me excited, so little direction now that basketball was over, and so little belief that everything was really worth it in the end.

And then in the bright darkness of defeat, as I felt my dream dying, the pain began to do its work. I felt the heartache of losing something that I loved, but at the same time, it became clear that maybe it wasn't so much about the end result as it was my journey along the way. I wasn't going to play for Kentucky, which meant my childhood dream was in shambles. Yet, the ride had been an incredible one, and the memories made combined with the lessons learned would eventually mean that the sweat and tears were worth it. I had learned to believe in myself and my gift. I had learned how to make others around me better and understand that it's not so much about winning or losing as it is living up to our potentials and doing what we can with what we've been given.

Maybe Elisha Justice didn't win. Maybe I gained something internally that couldn't be quantified on a scoreboard or a full-ride scholarship. And for now, that would have to do because it seemed like the right thing to do was start believing in a new dream.

6

One in a Million

Patience is the art of hoping.
—Luc de Clapiers

It was time to start believing in a new dream.

The end of March was a pretty depressing time. Coming up with a new dream wasn't easy after investing the majority of my life into the game of basketball, and I had no clue what I would be doing next year. I was about to just pick a school, flip a coin, or draw a straw and be done with it. I was not happy with God—like He had orchestrated some kind of divine trick to allow me to get so excited about a dream, be that close to obtaining it, and fall short right at the finish line. I figured I would just go to Asbury University and force myself to be content. Besides, I had grown up playing on this court, and I loved the school and the people there.

Of course, I couldn't bring myself to commit to a school and major in "being content," so I delayed making a decision even longer. In most cases that kind of procrastination is the death of ambition, but I felt something inside telling me to wait. There are many virtues that we admire in people that are marketable on résumés: love, joy, peace, kindness, gentleness, faithfulness, self-control. They all require something incredible to keep them consistently. But the most annoying one to be tested on is patience because it requires that you *do* nothing. Waiting is the worst. And this is exactly what I felt like in this period from March to April. I was giving up all control and trusting that something might happen, and I refused to take matters into my own hands and decide which school I would go to without knowing for sure that my first love's door was closing forever. I found solace in the stories of my biblical heroes, who, despite several glaring character flaws, definitely proved they could survive the patience test. If the Israelites could wait forty years in the desert, if Abraham could stick it out until he was one hundred years old to have his first son, and if Joseph could spend over thirteen years in prison for crimes he didn't commit, I should be okay.

And it wasn't terribly long before my dad called me and told me to expect a call from a Kentucky coach. Ha! I already felt as though God was pranking me with this whole wild ride, and now it seemed that my dad was also in on it. Then Coach Kelley pulled me out of class toward the end of the day and took me to his office. I sat down, anxious to know what he was going to share that required an exit from class.

"Okay, Jarrod, here's what's happening. First an update on Elisha Justice. He's talked to UK and told them that he's sticking with his commitment to Louisville."

"Really? Interesting," I replied, my heart starting to pump but trying to mask any premature excitement. After all, just because he wasn't going to UK didn't mean I had an open invitation. Kelley continued. "Jarrod, that spot on Kentucky could be yours. You're going to get a call from a coach soon, so be ready."

Unbelievable. There was no way this could be real. It seemed like an illusion, a desert mirage sent to tempt me, but surely this could not be happening.

Then after school my phone rang. Unknown number. Usually that meant I would send it to voicemail. Not today. I'd never seen my heart skip a beat at an unknown number.

"Hello?"

"Jarrod Polson?"

"Yea, it's me."

"This is Orlando Antigua, assistant basketball coach at Kentucky."

First I needed to change my pants.

Then, after talking with Orlando about their interest in me, I decided to play pickup with the team for a couple weeks to see if I belonged. And at this point, I felt ready for the challenge. Two years in a row my team had come pretty close to remaking the movie *Hoosiers*. My big fish prowess had earned me legendary status in my hometown. Everyone knew who I was, and it seemed like a done deal that soon I would be a lottery pick in the draft and bringing hope to nerdy-looking white kids all across the country. I was on top of the world ... a celebrity ... a household name ... a hometown hero ... a pretty big deal.

———

And it was with this backdrop of confidence that I entered the Craft Center (UK's practice facilities) with Coach Robic. He was giving me a personal tour one would expect as a recruit, but I still had no idea what was transpiring with the invitation to play with the team. The coaches had spelled nothing out at this point in terms of offering a spot on the team, and the feeling of mystery added to my suspicion that I was really asleep in my bed, enjoying the greatest dream of my life. We ventured into the weight room, where I met Rock Oliver, the intimidating strength coach. I felt

naked and judged as this man eyed me up and down with this
quizzical look on his face, wondering what business my 165-pound
frame could have entering into his domain. Coach Robic sent me
into the locker room to change and get ready to play.

It was a surreal moment to walk into that locker room. The
wooden lockers with the players' nameplates quickly caught my
eye. The ceiling demanded my attention; its circular metal banner
read, "As iron sharpens iron, so one man sharpens another." In
my mind's eye, this was a holy sanctuary—the inner sanctum of
the legends I idealized as a kid. This was where Jamal Mashburn
toweled off the sweat from his brow after a hard practice and
where Jeff Sheppard tightened his sneakers before stretching out
his calves. This was no place for an ordinary citizen, and I had a
respect for it. I knew I had to go in with the caution of a surgeon
entering the left ventricle for I was about to enter the soul room
of Kentucky basketball, the chamber that pumped blood into the
veins of the Big Blue Nation.

I found an unoccupied locker and stool to sit at, laced up
my scuffed red shoes (not a color that fit in well in my current
surroundings but the only basketball shoes I owned), and got
dressed to hit the court. This was also an out-of-body experience
because no one was really acknowledging my presence. The epic
characters around me were in their own world, in more ways than
one. I was surrounded by the likes of Patrick Patterson, Demarcus
Cousins, Eric Bledsoe, Darius Miller, and the list goes on. Of
course, I was a celebrity too, in Jessamine County, and had become
such a decorated high school athlete that the feeling of being a
nobody was completely foreign. I had made it so far, climbing this
ladder of success, and why shouldn't I join the ranks of the world's
best players? Rupp Arena had seen what I could do, and it seemed
natural this was the next step in my quest to become one of the
immortalized greats. In my daydream surrounded by future NBA

players, I was starstruck and in a trance. But suddenly, the silence was broken.

"Who the *bleep* are you?"

I followed the voice to its source: John Wall.

I didn't know what to say. My face was about as red as the shirt I was wearing. Being unknown was not something I was accustomed to. And here I was in the Kentucky practice facility experiencing one of the most confusing emotions of my life. On the one hand, someone had just asked a very valid yet humiliating question. On the other hand, my excitement skyrocketed. John Wall had just talked to me! I couldn't wait for the ensuing conversations. "Guys, you won't believe who talked to me today."

"Oh yeah? Who?"

"John Wall."

"*The* John Wall? What! What did he say!"

"Well, I can't repeat it."

It's a strange thing to be elated by the presence of one of your heroes, and the most popular man in the state of Kentucky, while at the same time completely humiliated by your interaction. I was clearly not in Jessamine County anymore. Perhaps the NBA lottery pick and Nike endorsements were further away than I had hoped.

This brief period of time was full of so much excitement and anticipation that much of it was a blur. But there are the things that you don't forget, those poignant moments of humility when you realize your talent that you previously regarded as elite is completely trumped by the talent of the next level.

At six foot two I was among the tallest on my team in high school, even by big man standards. I jumped for the tip-off in that world. In my new world, six foot two was small, even by guard standards. I looked up at Josh Harrelson, who was six foot eleven, and somehow convinced myself it would be a good idea to try and stop him from getting to the rim. I got dunked on quite emphatically, and that pretty well set the tone for these next two weeks during pick-up games. My old antics would no longer prove effective against this breed of players. I used to be a driver and slasher but quickly realized that was not going to work well in the land of giants.

Size wasn't the only thing to adjust to either. It would have been nice if being the smallest also meant I was the quickest. Not the case. It's one thing to watch John Wall and Eric Bledsoe on TV and a completely different thing to watch them matched up against each other playing pick-up ball right next to you. Their competitiveness and level of play was amazing, and my strategy had to adjust from how to successfully dominate as a point guard to how to minimize the number of times I looked stupid. Most of the guys I was running around with were going to be in the NBA in the next year or two, and here I was as a senior in high school trying to decide between schools like Transylvania and Liberty. This experience should have made me want to run a million miles away from that gym and toward a school like Transy. What was I to do with Demarcus Cousins waiting for me in the lane? I was scared to look at him the wrong way, let alone drive into the lane against him.

Needless to say, I did nothing spectacular out there during these games, but I never backed down and proved that I could keep up and belong out there. One play in particular I will never forget involved me making a move and swishing a pull-up jumper. Running back to the other side of the court, Demarcus Cousins said, "All right, this kid can actually play a little bit."

He would never remember that, but to me, it was water to my thirsty soul. Little things like that kept me going, kept me believing that there was hope. It meant so much because everything else about that period of time was pure intimidation. Even the Craft Center itself had an aura of greatness about it that seemed to subtly prohibit the weak from entering. The championship banners hanging up on the left side of the gym spoke for themselves. I stared at them in awe, remembering the names of those I idolized as a boy, marveling at how many years of dominance this program had spent building a dynasty. These victories, the banners, the championships, and the current players on the team all stood like grave monuments defending the excellence and tradition of Kentucky …

"Be great, or do not tarry here."

I felt that warning, but I didn't falter in my desire. This was what I had wanted so badly since I was a child. I had to have a chance at playing the sport I loved for the team I loved even more.

Pressure was building, and time was running out to make a decision for school. At this point so many people were asking me questions about what was going on, but the truth was I really didn't know. I didn't feel like I could choose because there really had been no offer. I just kept going to these open gyms assuming that I would hear at some point that the dream was just that: a dream. And it would be time to wake up.

I walked into the gym one day after school, and it was empty.

Great, I thought to myself. *Now they're not even calling me to let me know that open gym is cancelled. I might as well leave.*

But an inward nudge said, "Couldn't hurt to shoot for a few minutes."

I shot around for about ten minutes in complete solitude, each bounce echoing off of the walls and breaking the silence. Suddenly, Martin Newton, the director of basketball operations at the time, appeared in the doorway and walked over to me.

"Hey, can we talk for a few minutes?" he asked.

I said yes but immediately envisioned the conversation in my head before he said anything else. I expected the worst. "Kid, we've loved having you play with us, but you're not the direction we are looking to go." I wanted to prepare myself mentally for my strong, understanding, and composed response. Now that I was ready for the worst, I listened to what he had to say.

"Jarrod, I know you're probably feeling in the dark about where all this is going, so it's time to let you in on what the coaches are thinking. I've gotta tell you that they have liked what they've seen out of you. They're looking for someone who can run the scout team point guard, and they feel like you are capable of doing that. We can't guarantee you a scholarship or anything like that, but you are welcome to be a part of the team."

I was speechless. I never thought in a million years that the position of "scout team point guard" could sound so unbelievably flattering. Newton continued. "And, here's the deal. If a scholarship happens to become available, there is always a chance that you could earn it."

I did everything in my power to keep my composure. I had amped myself up to leave the building in the tears of defeat, and now I was preparing to leave with tears of joy. My huge smile pretty clearly communicated my answer, and I simply said, "Thank you. Thank you for this opportunity."

Before walking out of the Craft Center, I looked up at the banners one more time, realizing that the monuments of old were not holding up their arms in denial of my aspirations. They were welcoming me into the winningest program in college basketball's history. I couldn't believe it.

There was only one thing missing, the thing my brother Eric had told me all year to be expecting: a call from John Calipari. A few days later, his prophecy finally came true. I was out in the backyard shooting around with my sister Ashley and cousin Elle when the phone rang. It was a short conversation, but he expressed that he would love to have me as a part of the team. That's all I needed to hear.

There were so many obstacles, so many reasons why it was impossible, and even more doubt in my mind that this could really be a reality. I had been pretty upset for a while, disappointed that God could even allow me to get so excited about a dream that would never come to fruition. When I was in that moment, it was impossible for me to understand all the intricate details of *timing*. I could have allowed the fear of uncertainty and anger over not being given a quicker opportunity to force an accelerated decision into a school I didn't love. But had I taken matters into my own hands and made a quick decision to end the difficulty of being patient, I would have committed to a different program without allowing the path of my most-beloved school to open up. Plus, if my faith was going to prove authentic during this time of transition, I needed to learn to trust in God more than I trusted my own desires and plans. The best dreams are definitely worth working for, and this taught me they're also worth *waiting* for. Against all odds, I had become one in a million.

— 7 —

Be Careful What You Wish For

You may encounter many defeats, but you must not
be defeated. In fact, it may be necessary to encounter
the defeats, so you can know who you are, what you
can rise from, how you can still come out of it.
—*Maya Angelou*

I had accomplished the biggest and most outlandish dream of
my youth, and I don't want to downplay how lucky I felt. The
percentage of people who get to live out their dreams has got to be
astronomically low. A 2012 Gallup poll discovered that 52 percent
of American employees are "not engaged" at work, meaning that
"they're sleepwalking through their workdays, putting in time—
but not energy or passion—into work." Basically, over 50 percent
of all Americans don't like their occupations.

And here I was, putting in all my energy and passion into
what I longed for as a kid. What more could I want? Yet I would
be lying to you if I pretended that this long-awaited dream hadn't
rapidly escalated into somewhat of a nightmare. Or if nothing else,
a painful period not quite like I had imagined.

I officially joined the team so late that I didn't really get the red carpet rolled out for me. And since I was a walk-on, I couldn't even live with the team in the Wildcat Lodge. I could have, if I wanted to pay a lot of money for two months of living until the fall semester started. I already had to shell out some cash to pay for a summer class just so I could participate in the workouts with the team, so it seemed foolish to lose more money on the lodge, considering my home in Wilmore was within commuting distance from downtown Lexington. I drove there and back, there and back, and sometimes, there and back again. Maybe if I hadn't been driving so much, I could have been more in the loop with the team.

One Wednesday night I can easily recall my huge new world making me feel painfully small. I walked out of a huge lecture hall after night class ended into the fresh air between some huge trees on UK's huge campus. At least the people in this story didn't seem huge: I was with two guards on this huge Wednesday night, Stacey Poole and Brandon Knight. At least both were under six foot five tall. But their talent—huge.

"Man, how your legs doing?" Poole asked.

"Done! I can't believe how sore I am," Knight shot back.

I paused, a little perplexed because I hadn't done any workouts yet.

"What are y'all sore from?" I asked.

"The workouts we had last night and this morning were crazy! Our legs our dead."

"Aw man, that's tough," I said, trying to sympathize with them without letting on that I was humiliated for not even knowing the workouts happened, let alone that I wasn't there. What I wouldn't have given to take that leg pain and trade it in for the pain I felt internally from feeling so tiny.

The next day I went into the Craft Center and formally met the strength coach, Mike Malone. He had no clue who I was.

"I'm Jarrod Polson ... I just joined the team but don't know the schedule for workouts."

"Well, we've been lifting for a week, but get in here tomorrow. Here's a schedule," Mike said, filling me in.

Another embarrassing moment came a few weeks later when Mike decided to have us work out at the Nutter Complex, the domain of the football team. The running workout was scheduled at 4:00 p.m. It was up to the players to get there on their own on this particular day, so after a morning team lift, I traveled back to Wilmore to try and catch a quick nap. As always, I left extra early to give myself plenty of time to get warmed up and stretch but more importantly to follow the oldest walk-on rule in the book: *never be late*! I parked outside Commonwealth Stadium at three thirty and headed toward the football facility. As I walked inside, I noticed that it was completely empty, but being thirty minutes early, I decided to give it a few minutes. By three forty-five I started to get a little nervous, as still no one showed up, and by three fifty-five, I was in complete panic mode. I found a lady at the front desk and asked her if this in fact was the Nutter Complex, at which she said it was.

"However, there is also an outside field called Nutter as well, so you might be looking for that," the woman calmly said with a smile.

My heart sank as I sprinted as fast as I could to the field that I had now figured out we would be running at. On a day I showed up extremely early, I was three minutes late, and that was the last time I ever broke the walk-on rule again.

And these were the kind of occurrences that defined my first summer as a UK basketball player. I was "a part of the team" but at the same time, never really taken seriously.

Mike Malone may have done his fair share of making fun of the small, white, walk-on kid, but I will always be thankful to him for making me feel like I belonged a tiny bit in this huge world. It's easy to feel alone when you're living your dream because the difficult things that come up are hard for people you're close with to understand. From the outside looking in, I had nothing to complain about. Life was working out perfectly, just as I had always hoped. But in reality, I was learning the oldest cliché in the book: *be careful what you wish for.*

———

I returned home for the night after an average of three hours of driving each day. It was not unusual to watch ESPN while eating my favorite evening meal, a bowl of cereal. It was also not unusual for my dad to appear. His life is a force of consistency, an ever-present asker of questions, and someone who has always been and always will be there. He loves his kids as much as any father could and UK basketball as much as every native Kentuckian should. As you can imagine, this was naturally a time in life super-saturated by Dad's questions.

"So, how's it going?" he started, right as I was diving into my Cinnamon Toast Crunch.

"Good," I said between chews, trying to focus instead on the happy side of sports, like the top ten plays of the day. Anything to take the focus off of my miserable day.

"How's practice? Harder than high school?" he joked.

"Yeah, I guess," I answered in about as much depth as I could muster.

"You guess?"

"I'm just a walk-on ... I don't really go to practice."

"What ya mean?"

"Nothing. It's fine. It's just getting started next week. Just a lot of workouts right now."

"Hmmm…" Dad switched subjects, not giving up. "How about pick-up games? Aren't you guys getting a lot of action with those?"

"Yeah, I mean, they go a long time. Usually about two hours straight."

"That's awesome. How are those going? You showing 'em what you can do?"

"Yeah, I show 'em I can make uncontested layups."

"Oh, yeah! You coming away with some steals? I figured you'd have to impress them with your defense since they're not going to give you anything for free on the offensive end."

"Well, actually, that's not what I meant."

"Huh?"

"Well, there are eleven players on the team right now. That's great except that means when you run five on five, there's one man out. Somebody's gotta sit, and it's not gonna be a McDonald's All American. I basically shoot layups by myself on the side goal and watch the whole time."

"Oh, I see. Well, that's how it starts, right? Be patient and wait until your chance to show them what you can do."

"Yeah."

"You know, you need to be more assertive too. Maybe try pushing yourself in there to give people some rest once in a while. And when you're in, don't be afraid to score. You know, you can compete with those guys. They're human too, not just D-1 machines. You've got incredible floor vision and could really create some offense by being unselfish. You can show some of these all-stars what real point guard play looks like."

"Dad, I want to play. But it's ridiculous. These guys are sick. My best bet right now is working my tail off in the weight room, hustling during drills, and not be the guy who is going to come in and ruin the flow of the game by trying to be some Rudy story."

"I get that. I'm just saying that you've got a lot to offer out there even though it might not feel like it right now. You've got talent too, and they'll see it before long. You just need to get rid of the fear, take some shots out there, and prove to yourself that you can do it."

"I took some shots, Dad. The last game we played I got to come in while somebody needed a break. I usually just pass the ball as soon as I get it so I don't mess anything up. But eventually they started double teaming someone else on our team, leaving me wide open because they knew I wasn't going to do anything. They didn't even guard me. Like I wasn't even there. So I figured if they were gonna do that to me, I might as well take a few shots. But nerves got me. I could make those shots with my eyes closed in high school. I had two wide-open chances, and the pressure won. I bricked them both, and our team lost because of it." I paused, realizing the moment had gotten heavy as I introduced some vulnerability.

My dad thought for a minute, taking in the reality that I was really struggling and that this didn't seem like everything it was cracked up to be.

"Hey, it happens. You can't make 'em all. You've got to have freedom to fail if you want any hope of succeeding," he said, breaking the silence.

True, but I wasn't into a quick fix moral of the story. "Well, in my shoes, it doesn't feel like that. I'm already just a walk-on with no business on the court with these guys. I don't even get a schedule for workouts or get to live in the same place as the team. I'm basically a manager. And if that's not humiliating enough, when I do get in and get one chance to gain some respect, I make a complete fool of myself. I guess I just need to be happy with where I'm at as a walk-on and quit hoping for more."

I took the last bite of my cereal. I turned off the television. The room was quiet now, empty. The thing is, I didn't really have that conversation with my dad. He asked me all those questions. But I didn't give any of those answers. The things actually happened with the weights and pick-up games, but I didn't want to talk about them with anyone. How could I be whiny about the dream I had the privilege of living? I kept a smile on my face in my huge new world, but on the inside my mind-set was pretty screwed up. There were a lot of times when I just wanted to quit, wondering why I ever chose this path. The isolated incidents kept piling up, and the humiliation was becoming like everything else during this painful transition: huge.

— 8 ———————

Culture Shock

Sports have become a defining attribute
for men, unfortunately.
—*Joe Ehrmann*

I was raised in a family that drank vinegar for stomach ailments
and barely kept Tylenol stocked in the medicine cabinet. In fact,
there was no medicine cabinet. I think my mom kept the pills by
the coffee, the only other drug in the house. Doctors and antibiotics
were reserved for mortal injuries or deadly viruses. So I never
would have thought of communicating my blues to an outside
source to get my condition labeled, but after these two months, I
was ready for some antidepressants.

Luckily, in my depressed world I was not left completely
alone. A ray of light had been given to me so that I did not suffer
in solitude. Jon Hood was a teammate who went in those shoes
before me, who could not only understand the way I was feeling
emotionally but also help me with these foreign logistics to which
I was acclimating. Sometimes I would literally just follow him
around because he knew what he was doing and where we were

49

supposed to be. The bonus was that he was a fellow Kentuckian who didn't get much playing time the year before, so he also knew how I was *feeling*.

"Jarrod, we've got running at the track," and he'd take me.

"Pick-up time, Polson." And off we'd go.

I very well could have been an annoyance, yet he always gave me that great feeling that someone actually had my back and was looking out for me.

When I felt depressed, the worst thing about any of the circumstances was that feeling that no one could truly understand them. *Alone.* And no pill could take that feeling away. But Jon could empathize with me, and he did.

I had to guard Brandon Knight in practice, someone whose skill and athleticism were far above mine.

Hood understood.

I had gained ten pounds of muscle and added several inches to my vertical in that two months. And Knight could still leave me in the dust in a suicide.

Hood understood.

When I finally did get a chance in a pick-up game and the nerves made me miss an open shot …

Hood understood.

In high school I could almost always get to the rim and finish a layup or draw a foul. Not with the likes of Terrence Jones or Enes Kanter lurking in the paint.

Hood definitely understood.

When I was the eleventh man and had to watch pick-up games for hours on end …

Hood understood.

Now, interspersed between these depressing periods were some glimpses of light that kept me holding on, emotionally speaking. Coach Cal wanted to get us used to playing against older guys and some professionals. (He had no problem contacting both.) What better way than to gather some UK alumni and develop a platoon system so that each group would play five to ten minutes against the players of old? Unfortunately, I was the odd man out, so Calipari put me on the alumni team so I would at least get to be a part of the drill. While it wasn't ideal to be playing *against* my current teammates on the opposing side, I couldn't help but appreciate the opportunity to run the court with players like Ravi Moss, Erik Daniels, and Nazr Mohammad, who I looked up to while I was growing up.

Mixing things up like this also gave me a little bit of mental freedom from the fear of messing up. I played pretty well during those scrimmages and started remembering why I was in love with this game in the first place. I was having fun. And coaches began to notice.

During a practice our team came up with a steal and fed me the ball so quickly that the defense didn't have time to recover. I was all alone on a fast break. This is among the most exciting moments in basketball, when it's just you and the rim, a thousand creative possibilities, and expectant viewers on pins and needles waiting anxiously to see the most artistic showcases players are capable of. There's only one outcome that is unacceptable: missing a dunk. It's not an option. They had let my missed shots slide because they understood the battle with my nerves. But for the walk-on to have the audacity to go up for a dunk and be rejected by the rim? I could kiss my spot on the team good-bye. I needed to lay in the ball and guarantee my team the easy two points.

Dribbling somewhere between half-court and the free throw line, I changed my mind.

Planting both feet in the paint, I launched myself toward the rim, drew back the ball with my left hand, and slammed it home.

Tomahawk.

The whistle blew. Calipari had stopped the practice, and I was sure that I had broken some kind of unwritten rule. Maybe walk-ons aren't allowed to dunk.

"Time out! Was that, Jarrod? I might stop practice after that one!"

Now practice continued, but I couldn't help but smile when I saw the look of excitement on my coaches' and teammates' faces after that moment. They were beginning to see that there was more to me than meets the eye.

The basketball court wasn't the only place where I was experiencing culture shock. A minivan was the most-advanced form of transportation I had experienced growing up in Wilmore, Kentucky. And a big trip was defined as the annual family vacation to the Upper Peninsula of Michigan, where my grandparents owned a cabin on Piatt Lake. Seven people in a minivan for fifteen hours sounds like some people's version of purgatory, and that's not far from the truth. It was pretty awful. With five kid bladders there weren't enough exits on the interstate, so my mom developed a strategy of tossing a diaper over her shoulder any time she heard the familiar yelp, "I have to pee!" The adventures involving crying children, drive-through debacles, and car-top carrier explosions could merit their own novel.

You might think surviving that trip every year would have been ample training to prepare me for any kind of endeavor when it comes to travel-related stress. However, the prospect of flying was altogether terrifying. I was nineteen years old and had never been on a plane.

Luckily I had Hoody there as always to help me with all the tricks to traveling and how things would go down. What he couldn't express to me was the overwhelming experience of taking off on an airplane for the first time. We were headed to Detroit, which isn't any great length of time in the air. Of course, that doesn't change your take-off speed; it's still insane.

Settling into my chair and gripping the armrests, I stared straight forward after buckling my seat belt as tight as it would possibly hold me. Those turbines started humming, then screaming as our plane accelerated at an incredible rate. I was screaming, but only on the inside, as my stomach dropped out of me while the wheels lifted off the ground and we became airborne. I know it's way more likely that someone would die in a car crash than an airplane. But somehow that knowledge didn't make me feel better as the cars below grew smaller and smaller until they disappeared under the clouds, so incredibly lucky to be safely attached to the ground. The seat belt is a small consolation when you are thirty thousand feet above the earth's crust. Regardless, that thing stayed tightly wrapped around my waist until we landed safely in Detroit.

Flying was one thing I definitely needed to get used to, although I came to see why it was a favorable alternative to the minivan. I think my first flight lasted five minutes or so. And then it was time for another transition. Growing up in my family, it was a real treat to go out to McDonald's. If we were really lucky, Wendy's. My palate was extraordinarily simple and inexperienced, and the restaurant that Calipari took us to in downtown Detroit was unlike anything I ever seen. Seafood, steaks, pastas, and all sorts of stuff that you couldn't find at the Great Wall Chinese Restaurant in downtown Wilmore, Kentucky.

I was going to find the cheapest thing on the menu and go with that since that was my normal mode of operation in a situation like this. Plus, I was a walk-on, so I figured I probably shouldn't go wild, even if I had thrown down a tomahawk in practice. I could always see what other people ordered and then make my call after that. The waiter came around to Josh Harrelson.

"For you tonight, sir?"

"Yeah, I'll have this crab," Josh answered nonchalantly, pointing at the menu.

He just ordered a whole crab... I thought to myself. And this was while Harrelson was living behind the shadow of Enes Kanter, long before Josh conquered the mighty Jared Sullinger and Ohio State and became famous for his jorts. *In that case, maybe I'll have a steak*, I thought.

"How about for you?" Our waiter was giving me the go-ahead.

"I'm going to try the filet mignon."

I'm not even sure I said its name properly, but that steak changed my life. I never understood the big hoopla about steak until that fateful night. And I've been hooked ever since.

This new lifestyle was offering me all kinds of things that I had never tasted before. The plane ride gave me a feel of fortune. The steak changed my idea of good food. What was next?

It was time to travel to Windsor, Canada, for my first taste of fame.

These were exhibition games against teams no one's ever heard of for an inconsequential victory in a city 345 miles from Lexington. None of this deterred the sea of blue fans anxiously awaiting the tip-off. For once the prospect of sitting on the bench carried with it a certain perk in that I wasn't carrying any pressure on my shoulders during these warm-up drills. I knew I wasn't going to play any substantial minutes. Here I was, living my dream, suited up for the University of Kentucky and so close to the court that I could touch it. What beautiful misery to know I wouldn't actually *play* on it. Mentally, I could tease myself with the scenarios necessary for Cal to call my name. On a roster of ten players, I was just an ankle sprain away from some playing time. No, Jesus wouldn't want me thinking that way. Forget injuries. All I needed was for Brandon

Knight to raise his hand and admit that the pace of college play forced him to take a breather. Unfortunately for me, Brandon didn't know the meaning of the word *tired*.

But I would get my chance. There is an unwritten mercy rule that says you must play the walk-ons with a few minutes left if there is no chance they can mess anything up. The game went fast, and when we were up by several hundred points, Coach let me loose.

I shouldn't have been surprised that our quieted fans suddenly burst forth with a mighty uproar. I had seen this happen many times when the little guy who never gets to play goes in at the end of the game, but it was entirely different to *be that guy*. This was only the beginning of a relationship with the fans that I got to experience during the next four years of my life. I played well enough during my few minutes on the floor, scored four points and picked up a couple assists. Of course, something happened that day that was far more important than anything in the stat book: I had played my first game as a Kentucky Wildcat. Sure, it was against a team no one will remember in a country not accustomed to basketball, during a victory that had little significance in the grand scheme of the season. But none of this mattered, because for me this was a cosmic event. And I was about to learn that the universe took notice.

I decided to check my flip phone back at the hotel, and the poor little guy was completely overwhelmed. It was ready to explode with over one hundred texts from family, friends, and numbers I didn't know. I had never experienced anything like that before, and neither did I know how all of these people were even getting my number or what to do in response.

"Great game, Jarrod!" from an unknown number.

"Who's this?"

"Steve."

"Steve who?"

"Steve Stevens."

"*Ohhhhhhhh.* Thanks!" (Insert confused emoticon that insinuates, "How did you get my number?")

I didn't want to spend five hours on conversations that would go like that.

It was time to go where I could know who my true friends were: Facebook. Immediately over a hundred requests popped up with a hundred more notifications and messages congratulating me on the game and remarking about how incredible it was to see me on TV.

Now I knew what it felt like to witness the effect of the Big Blue Nation's powers in producing the feeling of fame. I liked the attention at this point since there were no strings attached, all positive energy, and it gave me the sense that I was somebody, that I had arrived. After all, I had just scored four points for Kentucky. Even better, Coach Cal told the radio post-game show that he was awarding me a scholarship and that I was "the most talented walk-on he had ever coached."

I may have felt alone at the beginning of the journey, but these surprises at the end of the summer were very timely in helping curb my bout with the blues. Granted, they didn't really treat the root of my problems, but they were nice distractions and gave me hope that this difficult journey would prove worth it in the end. Forget the meds. I would survive now on the food, fortune, and fame.

9

My First Season as a Kentucky Wildcat

Do not let what you cannot do interfere with what you can do.
—John Wooden

The red and blue lights flashed in the rearview mirror. I was on top of the world driving home from Canada, but the white minivan and I were still not above the law.

"License and registration, please," the Ohio police officer asked.

"Yes, sir," I answered, confident that I could find at least one of the two things he asked for.

"Kentucky, eh? You guys coming back from the Canada games?"

After asking more questions, and a brief period of waiting, I got off with a warning. Either that cop was a Kentucky fan, or a force field blocking speeding tickets was part of the scholarship package.

My life had been moving in the fast lane for the last two and a half months, so it seemed necessary that a police officer and a two-week break in Wilmore before the start of the school year would slow me down.

It was incredible to sit on the patio swing on our back porch and look out over the cornfields right behind our white fence. There is an amazing therapeutic and simple sense about the place where I grew up, and there was never a time I appreciated it more than those two weeks. I would need that foundation of peace and silence before heading into a school year filled with more noise than I could possibly imagine.

It began with Big Blue Madness. That name sounds like a hyperbole, but I assure you it is properly titled. People come and camp out around the Craft Center and the Wildcat Lodge for the week building up to the season's first open practice. Why would people live out of tents and play cornhole, jam on guitar, and toss the pigskin for a week? Besides the fact that this is probably how life is meant to be lived, there is the added bonus of free tickets to the Madness for those who brave the elements. It is also one of the rare times when players build friendships with the fans on a personable level. Sure, there were hours of autograph signings, but there was also time to goof off, get into the cornhole wars, toss the pigskin, or marvel at the genius who figured out how to set up a TV in his tent.

Some teams have a simple run-through that fans can come to at their leisure. At UK, it is more of a production than a practice, and as such, it is arguably one of the biggest events of the season. Before the team scrimmages against itself, there are the introductions. Having an announcer read each player's name as he rises from the bench to high-five his teammates is so twentieth century. At Big Blue Madness there is utter darkness, completely heightening all other senses for the cataclysmic array of lasers, fireworks, and dramatic videos heralding the dynasty of Kentucky basketball. This visual feast is compounded by thousands of people who have been building anticipation for seven days in their tents, waiting to unleash a barrage of screams that could easily have brought down the walls of Jericho.

I remember my name being called and stepping through a secret door, smoke coming up, and I made my entrance. The giant spotlight in my face blinded me to everything else, and it makes sense why so many players dance their way through the grand entrance. You *feel* like a rock star. Now, I had been a rock star in my Bob Cratchit days, but that required no dancing, so I just smiled and walked as fast as I could to the court.

I knew this would be one of the only times I would hear, "*Jarrrrrrrrrrrrrod Poooooooooolson!*" before a game since I wasn't expecting to get a real shot at playing, let alone starting. But I desperately wanted to do everything in my power to help the team. I had been given an incredible gift, and now that I was a scholarship player, I wanted to make sure the powers that be knew I was thankful. Thankfulness came easy now with the transition to actually living with the team in the Wildcat Lodge. Strictly from a practical standpoint, it was like my life was visited by the logistics fairy. The previous summer I spent all my free time driving back and forth to practices of which I never knew the times to join a team for which I never knew if I belonged. Now I didn't have to worry about being in the dark about workout times. It became legal for me to eat with the team, I wasn't late to conditioning because I couldn't find a football field, and I got to be a part of the dorm life with the team. Most importantly, I was starting to feel like an actual part of the team. If only I felt like there was a way to help my beloved team without actually being on the court.

———

And then, the box appeared. I opened it up to find all of my textbooks for classes, organized and ready to go. This was my ticket.

It wasn't necessarily written in the contract for my scholarship, but as everyone knows, if you're not going to get much playing time, you better do really well in school. My freshman year, this was the task I latched on to as the easiest and most obvious way I could help out. I had just finished high school with a 4.3 GPA, so I thought this would be no problem. And let's be honest, academics probably held a higher significance for my future. I had to be at 8:00 a.m. classes every day to do my fifteen credit hours, another eight hours of time with a tutor, and finally eight hours of study on our own time.

Growing up dreaming of playing at UK, spending thirty-one hours a week in class or studying was not a part of my vision. It was definitely no fun, but I bit the bullet and did it. There was a major transition happening in my life that was painful but incredibly good for me. I could no longer lead with my talent, but I could lead with my choices.

I was in a world dominated by talent. And though I did fine academically and learned a lot about the value of hard work and discipline, that didn't result in any miraculous amounts of playing time my freshmen year. There were the occasional blowout games where I could get a few minutes at the very end. And then along the way, there were a couple of surprises.

The first came against North Carolina in Chapel Hill, which happened to be our first big challenge of the season. It was a Saturday game played at high noon. That's a great time to watch a game and a terrible time to *play* one. We were slow, lethargic out there on the floor, like we would rather be taking a nap than playing basketball on national television. And when you're tired, the coach knows because you foul like crazy. During one of the time-outs, he spent the entire minute and a half playing detective.

"You guys are playing lazy! What kind of defense are you playing out there? Looks like somebody took a nap."

Heads all went down. Eye contact was lost. Coach Calipari was on to something. According to him, taking a nap before a game was one of the unpardonable basketball sins.

"Jones, did you take a nap?" Cal asked Terrence. He stared forward with those intense dinosaur eyes, hoping Cal would go around the circle and ask each player, then have a fair trial.

Cal kept digging. "Doron, did he take nap?" Ouch. Now he was going to Jones's roommate.

Doron Lamb was from Queens, New York. You don't come from Queens and not know that snitches get stitches. He avoided the question. The whole thing was almost becoming comical, like a scene from an elementary school where a young accessory to a crime doesn't want to tattletale on his friend. There was no direct confession of the crime, but that wasn't necessary. There was enough corroborating evidence to prove Jones's guilt.

On this year's team, Jones was not a leader defined by his position in the post, but his attitude and intensity usually acted as the team's thermostat. And the atmosphere had been set the perfect temperature to induce foul trouble.

By the end of the tight game, Terrence Jones, Doron Lamb, Brandon Knight, Deandre Liggins, and Josh Harrelson had either committed four fouls or had already been forced to sit out with five. We found ourselves in overtime against these tenacious Tar Heels, down one point with five seconds to play when Dre' fouled out. Now coach was in a real conundrum. North Carolina was shooting bonus free throws, and Coach walked down to the end of the bench to make a choice between me and Stacey Poole. He looked at me, then at Poole, then back at me.

"Go!"

I sped to the scorer's table and checked into a game in the Dean Dome in overtime with five seconds left, and I'd been on the bench the whole time. No pressure.

The first free throw found its mark, but the second banged off the rim into the hands of Darius Miller. And of all people, he threw the ball straight to me. It is impossible to describe the pressure in that moment other than to say that the bodily fluid running down my legs was not sweat. I took a dribble. Three seconds. Time froze as I faced our basket from the other side of the court. Carolina scrambled to set up their defense without fouling. The cats spread the floor, looking for a spot for an outlet pass. I had a choice to make. I could dribble a couple times, launch a bomb, and save the day for my beloved team, hoping my talent would come through as my three-point prayer splashed through the nets, immortalizing my name in the UK hall of fame. Or I could make a choice to be selfless, acknowledge the mathematical odds that my end-game heroics were not in my favor, and pass the ball up court to someone who had a better chance by being closer to the goal. I chose the second option—partly out of selflessness but also out of self-preservation. There was the soul-crushing fear of knowing that if I missed that shot, I'd be burned alive.

I zipped the ball up to Doron Lamb, of Queens, which not only meant he was no rat but also that he could handle the pressure. He was racing down the right side of the court and launched his half-court missile at the buzzer. The Dean Dome exploded with joyous celebration as the Hail Mary went far left.

I realize the only stat I accumulated in that game was five seconds of playing time, but to be a part of the action during those circumstances, chosen to go in with the game on the line, trusted to touch the ball under that dire a situation—all of that was enough for me. I was a part of the team. I belonged. And thanks to the nap situation, now I was Terrence's new traveling roommate.

I got another taste of the action against Florida, which became the same song but a different verse. No one was condemned for taking a nap this time, but we were back in foul trouble, and it was only the first half. I was put in the game and got a pass when the shot clock was winding down. Instead of taking the midrange jumper, I made the dumb decision to take a pro hop into the lane for an attempted layup. Chandler Parsons, who is now on roster with the Dallas Mavericks, came out of nowhere to spike my shot into the fourth row. That was embarrassing.

A couple minutes later, I came up with a loose ball. There were only five seconds left in the first half, so I had to speed down the court. I did a crossover to shake one defender, and then it was just me and one more Florida player to beat. I went up for the buzzer-beater layup, and it got pinned into the backboard and the rim and just stuck there. Another opportunity to make some noise was met with a kind welcome from the athletes of Division 1 basketball.

The whole season was pretty much a blur. I wasn't the only one who had some lessons to learn. Our team as a whole struggled a lot on the road, but we managed to make a deep tournament run after beating the overall number one seed, Ohio State. Josh Harrelson made a name for himself in playing a great game against Jared Sullinger. Harrelson will go down in history as the guy who pegged Sullinger in the chest to save the ball from going out of bounds. Then we went on to beat North Carolina and get our revenge from earlier in the season. We made it to the final four that year, falling short in the semifinal game against UConn. It was incredible to be a part of this magical season, culminating in a March Madness where "jorts" became the most popular article of clothing in Kentucky. I also got some TV time, not on the court but during our celebration after beating North Carolina and heading to the final four. At the beginning of the season I was too nervous, too out of my element, too afraid to dance when my name was called on a roster of a team I was still trying to see if I fit into. By the end of the season, I was caught on national television doing the "dougie" with a huge grin on my face.

It was a really hard transition from being the star on my high school team to being the very last player on the bench. The year before I was the one hitting game-winning shots and carrying our team through the tournaments. Now I was watching Brandon Knight hit game winners.

During my freshman year, the outlook I had on success in basketball had completely changed from high school. We lost the game, but we were learning lessons about how our little decisions affected the whole team. Ultimately, it was just an incredible blessing to feel as though I belonged. I didn't score many points, but I was part of a team that I cared about immensely, and I did whatever I could to make *them* better, whether that was on the court or off. Of course, I still had the itch to add more to my stat line than just minutes.

Photo by Chet White: UK Athletics

Luckiest layup of my life

My dad was more excited than I was

Ice cream, glasses, and my little sister.

Photo by (Samuel Delong

12th Region Champions: A memory I will never forget

The good ol' days

Photo by Samuel Delong

Last moment of my high school career

"I have learned to be content in all situations"

Photo by Brittany Macintosh)

Be your brother's keeper

Photo by Michael Huang

The family has grown!

— 10 ——————

Sophomore Slump

Consider it pure joy, my brothers, whenever you
face trials of many kinds, because you know that
the testing of your faith develops perseverance
—*James 1:2–3 NIV*

My sophomore year would be my time to shine. This would be the year that my hard work would pay off, and I would be able to show the world that I didn't just belong on UK's basketball roster; I belonged on the court. I had a year of experience under my belt. I had arrived at a state of belonging on this team, my confidence no longer hung on by a thread, and during the off season, I had made it my goal to get stronger and faster. I worked hard, and accomplished that mission. My whole life I had been the scrawny white kid with glasses, but at this point in my career, I gained some muscle and definition. I actually looked the part now. At least I thought so.

The timing seemed right as well since our team was undergoing a dramatic overhaul. Brandon Knight, Josh Harrelson, and Deandre Liggins all took their talents to the next level, leaving a vacancy in the point guard role. At a normal school when a team makes a run at the championship and then loses three starters, that means the next year is a rebuilding year with lowered expectations from the fans. Of course, Kentucky is no normal school. The term *rebuilding* has been replaced with *reloading*. And my sophomore year, the bullets we reloaded happened to be of the highest caliber. The player ranked number one overall coming in from high school: check (Anthony Davis). The number-two player overall joining our roster: check (Michael Kidd Gilchrist). The best point guard in the class, coming from an NBA pedigree family: check (Marquis Teague). And there was this tall, goofy-looking kid from Oregon who decided to commit as well, but we will get to him later.

The era of overwhelming talent would continue for another year, so maybe it was foolish to believe that this could be my year. However, though we had the quality, we were lacking in quantity, and when we had the beginning of the year cookout at Coach Cal's house, he gave me a dose of intoxicating optimism during our individual meeting.

"We are short on guards this year, so you're going to have to be ready to play some."

This sealed the deal. It was official. I was going to get substantial minutes on a team that had all the right tools to win a national championship. I might not have been the most talented person on the team, but I was a sophomore, which meant I had experience. I had to be the only point guard in history to play two seasons under Calipari. This had to be my year, our team's year, and the Big Blue Nation's year for all things to come together. Right out of the gate, we beat a very solid Kansas team in Madison Square Garden, and we were proving that the overall number-one ranking for our team was not unwarranted. We had what it took, and the time was coming for me to prove that *I* had what it took to help make this team end up with a ring.

We were up by thirty or forty points (at this point, who's counting?) against a smaller Division 1 opponent in Rupp Arena, and Coach put in all of the bench players with about three minutes remaining in the game.

"*Shoot!*" the familiar chants from the crowd began. But this was no time for a circus performance for the crowd. My goal was to go in and give 110 percent. The only audience I was concerned about was the coaches because I wanted them to see how serious I was about playing. This was going to be about more than getting minutes. I was on a mission to add substantial numbers to my stat sheet.

I did just that.

In those three minutes, I had two turnovers and missed a field goal attempt, and I got beat on defense while allowing my man to score on me. In those three minutes, our lead dwindled down to twenty. I don't know what happened to me out there, other than that the pressure I put on myself ended up creating a mountain of nerves that I couldn't conquer. It was unbelievable how disappointing my performance was, like I was cursed by some form of black magic. Murphy's law states that if it can go wrong, it will. I believed in Murphy after this game. Heading into the locker room, I hoped that maybe by some miracle the whole thing would go unnoticed. After all, the fans didn't seem to condemn me, and we still won the game by twenty points. Maybe the coaches all went to the bathroom at the same time during those three minutes, and the whole thing could just be forgotten and I'd get a second chance. Unfortunately, Murphy wouldn't have that. He showed up at the post game.

"Starters, really good game," Coach Cal said. "We played good defense, but we still have to improve on ..."

Everything was good so far, as long as he would keep talking about the starters.

"Now, Coach Robes, KP, Orlando, make sure I never play those guys at the end of the game again. That was embarrassing."

Okay, I would admit that. At least the negativity was directed at the group and not specifically at me.

"Jarrod, I don't even know what's wrong with you. I got nothing to say to you, kid."

I showered and got dressed in the locker room that night feeling completely defeated. I had worked so hard and set my expectations as high as they could go, only to be embarrassed in front of twenty-four thousand fans. More importantly, I had failed in front of Coach. That night I lay in bed until 6:00 a.m., completely restless and unable to fall asleep. Every time I put my head on the pillow, I had flashbacks of turning the ball over or missing a shot. I couldn't shake it. I had no idea that sadness and anger could give you physical pain until that night. I had a legitimate stomachache caused by my emotions, and I felt completely hollow.

I needed something to take the edge off, get my mind focused on the positive. I thought I would check my phone in hopes that a family member or friend would come through with some timely encouragement. Nothing. I ventured into the more impersonal world of Twitter, believing that maybe the world of cyber anonymity could deliver a dose of sympathy. Bad idea.

"LOL Polson sucks."

"Never play Polson again!"

There was no escape from the voices inside my head, and now unfortunately the voices of the world were in unison with the negativity within. I finally just turned on the TV in hopes that the sound could blur everything else out. That didn't work either, so I tossed and turned for six hours until the strain left me mentally exhausted and I finally fell asleep.

The next day I convinced myself that the past was the past and that I was going to have a fresh start. I got to practice extra early so I could get an hour of shooting in before practice started. Coach Robes happened to be in the gym, and he volunteered to rebound for me.

At first, it was just me and him. I was feeling pretty good, getting a nice workout in to relieve some stress and anger that I had battled all night. About ten minutes later, Coach Cal walked through the practice center doors. That was odd. He usually never came down that early. He walked over to the far side of the gym where I was shooting, said nothing at first, just watched. Was he going to watch me make a shot, see my perfect form, acknowledge my getting there earlier than anyone else to make myself better, and then take back what he said yesterday? He watched a few shots and broke the silence.

"You know, all of the players that ever played for me have always gotten better. But I think you have gotten *worse*."

Boom! I did not see that coming. I was already tired, defeated, and against the ropes. This punch was enough to take me out. I had no response.

"What do you think, Robes?" Cal asked.

Robes passed the ball back out to me for another shot. "I think he's scared, Coach."

They kept talking for a couple minutes, and I kept shooting. I had nothing to say. I had some thoughts but nothing to say. My first thought was to grab the ball, chuck it at Coach's face as hard as I could, and walk out of that place forever. Instead, I merely took pleasure in the idea and kept going through my drills, taking all of my anger in without saying a word.

About a half hour later the team gathered in the film room to watch some of the footage from the game the night before. Usually we never watched the last "scrub minutes," because we didn't have time, but today was different. We watched far enough to see a few of my bonehead mistakes, and after shaking his head, Coach Cal said, "Golly, turn it off. I can't take it. Jarrod, do you even belong on this team?"

An awkward silence took over the room for a few seconds. I had nothing to say. My teammates couldn't muster any words for me either. Not that they needed to. It was obviously a hypothetical question that didn't need an answer. A flood of self-doubt rushed through my mind, and I felt like I was right back where I had started during my first summer on the team. I tried coming up with a bunch of different excuses in my head, but none of them eased the torment or made me feel any better.

I had always let my confidence come heavily from the opinions of others, so these comments were particularly crushing. In these moments, I was tempted to let anger and hatred consume me for the way I had played and the response I got from my coach. But in hindsight, this was exactly what I needed to hear. They may have seemed like nasty comments without any purpose other than to completely tear me down. But now I believe that Coach knew exactly what he was doing. One of the noblest things I respect about Cal is that he genuinely cares about his players with all of his heart. He is not afraid to do whatever he has to do to get the best out of us, even at the risk of seeming intense or mean. He always preached to his players that they must have confidence in themselves and not let any other person's opinion change that. I had always leaned on the crutch of others' praise and allowed them to build confidence in me. Now he was taking away that luxury and teaching me a lesson that his confidence, or lack thereof, meant nothing. It was my own confidence that was the key. It is safe to say that this moment in time was rock bottom for me in terms of my basketball career. My coaches in the past had trouble enough raising my confidence enough for me to be able to play well, and even my brother had to feed my ego in elementary school when most kids are gleaming with cockiness. But this was a totally different situation. Coach Cal was using tough love, something I desperately *needed* but didn't necessarily *want*. And while I hated it at the time, it was crucial for my progress as a player and a person, and I am forever grateful to him for that.

— 11

Two Coins

Whatever you do, work at it with all your heart, as working for the Lord, not for men.
—Colossians 3:23 NIV

One night I lay awake in my bed at the lodge, forfeiting sleep to endure the familiar internal wrestling match as I struggled with what to do about my future at Kentucky. Staring up at the blank white ceiling, surrounded by the blank white walls, I seemed pretty blank and white to myself. I was completely torn about what I wanted. I don't know if there was an angel on one shoulder and a demon on the other, but I do know that there were two distinct voices in my head competing for my will.

"Jarrod, you're at your dream school. Just suck it up and be happy. Who cares if it's hard, humiliating, and hurtful?"

"But Jarrod, aren't you sick of being a victory cigar? You know you have what it takes to compete out there. You need to keep busting your chops so you can get a shot as a real contributor."

"No, you need to *accept* the fact that the contributions you're destined to offer are going to be encouraging your teammates, making them better in practice, and boosting the team GPA."

"But I feel like I can do more than that. I think I could run the point at this level and be successful."

"Jarrod, remember your performance the last three minutes you played? Remember how embarrassing it was to lay it all on the line, try your best, and then have the world laugh at you? Think of how much easier it would be to simply sit the bench, throw up inconsequential three-point bombs, and quit caring. You'll be truly free when you quit caring about doing more."

"But I can do more than that. That was one game. A terrible game. It happens, but it doesn't have to be what *keeps* happening."

"I'm just telling you: be content with your role. You're living your dream of being on Kentucky's team. Take some glory in being one in a million, practice your dance moves for when the starters win a championship, and stop trying so hard."

"I would, but I'm missing something."

"Yes. You're missing out on sleep. Now quit stressing out and wake up tomorrow happy you're on this roster."

"My dream wasn't to be on a roster. It was to *play* basketball at Kentucky, not to make it onto the team only to have my coach tell me that I'm getting worse. I'm not going to be happy sitting the bench for two and a half more years."

"What's the point of trying harder? You're competing with NBA players for playing time. You could live in the gym, work out all night, and major in basketball, and you're still not going to be faster than Marquis Teague. No matter how hard you work, you won't be able to jump higher than Michael Kidd Gilchrist. If you're not going to be the best, don't try. It will be a waste of energy. It would be better for you to offer nothing at all than to work yourself to death and come up short, get second place, and get no playing time anyway. Just think about the end result, and remember that if it isn't going to make a big difference, it is probably a waste of your time. You don't want to kill yourself just for more humiliation and less playing time."

Looking up at that blank wall, that answer seemed to ring true. If I was going to be happy, I needed to realize my humble role, not try so hard, and be content on the cheerleading team. The pressure would dissipate, and I wouldn't have any more sleepless nights. I wouldn't make myself do extra workouts before or after practice. I wouldn't have to try as hard in practice guarding players who were way better than me. I could simply accept my role as the kid who wasn't very good and go on with life. Still staring up, I took a deep breath and exhaled slowly. My eyes followed a crack on the wall and took my mind down a philosophical rabbit trail.

"Wait a second, Jarrod. Think for a second about where this line of thinking takes you. Will the choice make your life easier? Sure. Will it require less of you? Of course. But in the end, giving less will not do your heart justice."

I began to think about people I knew who exemplified the simple beauty of doing what they could with what they had, regardless of whether the world would sing their praises or write books about them. First I thought of our janitor who worked the night shift in the craft center. We would come in for a 6:00 a.m. workout, and there he was. Every day. He would do the most mundane job in the universe over and over again but always with a smile on his face. Some days, he would sing. What did he have to sing about? His work wasn't earning him any great pride, he wasn't breaking any records, and the salary can't have been setting him up for a lavish retirement. And yet, he still gave 100 percent of what he had.

And here I was, living my dream. Every circumstance in my life was perfect by the world's standards. My meals and schooling were paid for, so I never had to worry about money. I was on the best basketball team in the nation but still got to live right down the street from my family. I now knew how good filet mignon was and had even gotten to taste the thrill of being a minor celebrity in the Big Blue Nation. I had *everything*. And yet, I wasn't singing. My résumé was far more substantial, but this janitor's soul was much more alive. I was befuddled by how this could be the reality when I had so much in comparison to what I assumed he had.

Suddenly now my thoughts went to the biblical narrative of the poor woman giving two pennies in the offering plate at church. In the midst of the movers and shakers of the community who were writing big checks and raising the eyebrows of the members who observed their gifts, Jesus noticed this lowly woman. She was not impressive based on the results that she provided. She didn't have the building named after her, or sponsor the Israelite soccer team, or get a substantial tax write off that made her giving *worth it*. Her two cents was the smallest offering in the building that day, and yet Jesus praised her.

"You see that woman? In the eyes of God, she just gave more than anyone else. They didn't sacrifice anything with their gifts. But she put in all she had."

Suddenly my thinking was shifting. I had been so focused on what *I thought I needed* that I wanted to be sure my effort produced the fruit I was after. But it turns out that the size of the gift, or the talent, or what you receive as a result isn't the most important thing. It's the heart behind the gift.

I thought of my dad. His consistency is a mountainous marvel, working twelve hours a day without complaining about the work he doesn't love. But he loves his family. And he gladly provides for them by what he can do, even though there is no earthly glory for his sacrifice. In fact, he often goes unappreciated by the very children he supports, as evidenced every year at Christmas. Gifts would be torn open, followed by the shrills of joy and then the inevitable "Thanks, Mom!" even though Dad's check clearly paid the bill.

My mom must also have grasped the story of the two pennies in her own way because her life also inspires me. Her vocal talents were enough to woo the crowds at our megachurch, but she never allowed her talent to pull her away from raising her children. And although the applause of eight thousand people will elate anyone's pride, I swear Mom got more satisfaction singing for six with the family gathered around the piano for "O Holy Night."

And then there's my grandpa, who was blessed with not only the strongest forearms you will ever see but more importantly an overly generous heart. He has spent his entire life using the intelligent business mind God gave him to simply help people in any way he can. (It also helps that he married the most caring and gentle-spirited woman I've ever met.)

Whether you believe in God or not, I hope you agree that every person has been given a gift. And we all have to decide whether we will open them up to the world and work at them or take the easier road and let them sit there without giving our all. God reminded me during this difficult time of decisions that while we don't get to choose which talents and skills we get, we do get to choose how we use them and how hard we work to develop them. This was the point in my life where I decided if I was going to use basketball for a greater purpose or let it keep using me.

———

And like all difficult decisions, making the right one often requires that someone give us a push. For me, that person was Kenny Payne. He is one of those two-penny people, an assistant coach who doesn't get near the credit he deserves for the success of the Kentucky program. KP, as the players call him, is very instrumental in skill development. If you want to improve your game, he is the guy to call. I was committed at this point to keep working on my gift, accept the God-given talent I had received, but also to do my part. I was ready to work. And I knew I needed help, so he was the man I would turn to.

There was also Kyle Wiltjer, the goofy kid I promised I would come back and explain later. Kyle came all the way across the country from Portland to challenge himself against the best players in college basketball. He certainly was improving his game, but like me, he was also frustrated with playing time propositions. He was averaging ten to fifteen minutes a game, which was nice, except that he knew he could be starting and getting thirty-plus minutes at just about any other college in the country. Kyle and I approached Coach Payne together, as a unit, in hopes that the two-player proposal might be more appealing to KP's time.

"Coach, we gotta talk to you about something."

"Go ahead, shoot."

"KP, we want to get better. We both know we have more to offer this team than we are right now, but we need to work harder to make that possible."

"Okay, makes sense. What did you have in mind?"

"We know you've got a lot going on and have a lot of high-priority athletes that you're working with, but could we just work out with you before practices every day?"

"If that's what you think it will take, I'm willing to be here before practice."

Kyle and I were thrilled that he agreed. Then again, we had no idea what we had just asked for. KP killed us. This was no simple warm-up routine, and he lived up to his strenuous reputation of not holding back. By the end of each workout, we were drenched in sweat, our legs were killing us, and we were completely out of breath. We would go change our shirts and take a few minutes to fill our lungs with oxygen before the real practice started. It was grueling, but it was exactly what we needed. Now we were truly giving *our* two coins to the team.

––––––––––

Ironically, as these workouts became our new routine, it seemed that the difference they made was worth about two cents. I would say that nothing good seemed to come out of them, but that wouldn't be true. It was worse than that. It seemed like the more we gave, the worse things got.

During the middle of our SEC schedule, our team began functioning at its highest level, and most of our opponents couldn't compete. There were a lot of blowouts. Naturally, this meant that there was a pretty good chance I would have no choice but to go in at some point and redeem my blunders from the beginning of the season. Three games in a row, we were winning by around thirty points, and Cal would send me to the scorer's table with three or four minutes to go. And three games in a row, in the last three or four minutes, there wasn't a single dead ball, timeout, bleeding player, fire in a bathroom, or Geico commercial that stopped the clock.

I literally just sat at half-court with my warm-ups pulled off until the final buzzer went off. As comical as it sounds now, this was extremely embarrassing for me and felt like evidence that I was really under some kind of curse this season. Patience is so difficult when you are doing everything in your power, giving all that you have, and not seeing any results reassuring your efforts. It would be awesome if our best decisions reaped immediate change in our lives and life became immediately harmonious as our wills dictated a string of perfect circumstances.

However, this was not the case. So while Kyle and I killed ourselves getting stronger only to see a *decline* in our playing time (fourteen minutes sitting at the scorer's table is like a player's purgatory—far worse than years on the bench), it made sense that we stayed up late in our rooms talking about how incredible it would be to transfer to other schools.

We talked about being teammates and going to Stanford, running the pick and pop to perfection, or heading to Gonzaga and leading the team to a national championship. These conversations were not thought about with any actual seriousness, but we couldn't help but think how easy it would have been to run away to another location, leaving our problems behind and fixing life forever. However, I knew that my heart belonged at Kentucky, and the scenarios we dreamed about would remain for me just that— escape mechanisms.

There were other things that helped me escape the pressure I felt. It came from the unlikeliest source but involved quirky imagination and some cinematography. Kyle, Jon, and I recruited Robbie, Allen, and Matt to be part of the project. We were shooting around in the gym one night, and we thought it would be funny to make a video that made fun of ourselves. We stayed up all night working on it, and the joy of the WBA (white boy academy) was born. The Christmas song was particularly successful and brought me back my Troy Bolton-like roots. It was a great time and increased our social media prowess, and mostly, it was just a nice way to unwind and take basketball a little less seriously.

Of course, these creative escapes could never solve my main problem long-term. I was still somewhat of a timid puppy when it came to my self-confidence, no matter how much I prayed and hoped that I could shake the negative voices that had been a broken record in my head since my three-minute debacle. No amount of self-talk or solitude could get me mentally believing in myself at full capacity. I needed someone to speak confidence back into my broken psyche. And Kenny Payne became that person. When it seemed like no one else believed in me as a player, KP would always communicate that he knew I could compete and had talent. I know for a fact that I wouldn't have done the things I did at UK in my junior and senior seasons if it hadn't been for him working me out and instilling the confidence back into me that I desperately needed. He was always there to talk or push me on the court, even though "working out the walk-on" wasn't necessarily in his job description.

━━━━━━━━

It seems that prayer is rarely answered as we expect. I had hoped God would hear my pleas for confidence and magically instill a robust ego that would give me the courage to take risks on my convictions. And yet, no magic wand was waved. I didn't see my basketball number in the clouds with a big smiley face next to it or have a lifelike dream that Calipari came groveling to me with apologies and professions of my greatness. There was no blatantly divine miracle that changed everything in a fairy-tale instant. Instead, the answer to prayer came as it normally does—through another human being who was willing to give his two cents for a little dreamer named Jarrod.

— 12 ————————

National Champions!

*I wish everyone could get rich and famous and everything
they ever dreamed of so they can see that's not the answer.*
—Jim Carrey

had never worked harder or committed myself more fully to
anything in my entire life than I had in taking the plunge with
KP and working my tail off so that I might have a chance at getting
some playing time.

My reward? Front-row seats to one of the greatest basketball
teams ever engineered. People paid good money for seats like mine.
In fact, somebody paid $10,000 to sit behind me for the Kentucky
versus Indiana game that year. I just paid with blood, sweat, and
tears. I rode the bench and internally writhed with turmoil while
our team was having a season for the history books. Oh, the irony.

My outstanding memory of personal glory for me that year
came from an unlikely source: on a road game during the SEC
tour, where basketball is mostly a commercial break until these
schools can get back to the sport that really matters—football.

Regardless, I will never forget what happened down in South

Carolina. We were abnormally pumped up for this game and ended up winning the contest by a small margin of fifty points. I'm not sure exactly what caused the fire for us that day, but I do know some of it was because the Gamecocks' lair was more full of blue than it was red. It was special for many of the new players because it was their initial realization of how supportive and huge the Big Blue Nation really was. It was no surprise to me, but I did get a memorable dose of love in Columbia that I'll never forget.

The lane was open, and there were no defenders between me and the rim. My endorphins peaked as I cut toward the hoop, calling for the ball. The setup was perfect. The pass was bounced hard off the floor, and I just knew that gravity would be pulling it back down from its ascent right in front of the rim. I jumped hard off of two feet, rotating a full 360 degrees while catching the ball perfectly with my left hand. Time froze, and every pupil in the building dilated to a full eight mm as my brain recalibrated, my eyes found the rim, and I slammed it home.

The crowd exploded with oohs and ahs as I had just performed the dunk of my life. With a smile on my face, I jogged over to my seat on the bench. The whistle blew and the music started pumping in the stands, signifying that the announcer was about to introduce starting line-ups. Warm-ups were over.

And there you have it, folks. The highlight of my sophomore season was during layup drills off of a pass from Coach Robic. It won't be on any stat line, it wasn't on TV, and most of my family didn't witness it. Yet Robes, who was sarcastic by nature, even had to give me props.

But I was working way too hard for my only consolation to be a coach's compliment on a dunk in warm-ups. It was a year of dying to self. As a follower of Jesus that is meant to be a daily thing ... but it's much more convenient to die to yourself once and get it over with.

What I needed was to stop obsessing about my work and the desired results and learn how to take pleasure in the accomplishments of others. And there was probably no place with more opportunity to do that than having front-row season tickets to the 2012 national championship team. People often ask what it was that made this team so special, so dominant.

Theory number one: defensive dynasty. The old cliché that defense wins championships proved quite true. That road win against South Carolina was a good example—you beat a team when guards dribble down into the paint and make eye contact with Anthony Davis or Terrence Jones and then wisely retreat back to the three-point line. This theory also found support during the North Carolina game at Rupp Arena. Most nail-biters are won on a last-second shot. Anthony won this game on a last-second block.

This leads nicely into the second theory of why this team was so great: Anthony Davis himself. I will admit that I've never played with anyone who had a higher level of impact on the game, so people's assessment that he was just a freak of nature is warranted. But it was not always so. At the beginning of the year when we played against Transylvania, he had real trouble scoring. Then KP got ahold of him, and I witnessed how much AD put into his workouts that year. He definitely had talent, but he wouldn't be where he is today after leading UK to a championship if he hadn't made the choice to develop his skills every day. I got the opportunity to see a player who had no offers of significance from colleges during his junior year in high school become the MVP on a national championship team for Kentucky two years later.

The third theory is quite plain, but probably the most truthful, this team simply *hated* losing. And it only happened twice that whole year, so when the lightning struck, it was memorable. The first came at the hands of the Hoosiers in sacred Assembly Hall.

It was a five o'clock game, so students had all day to "prepare" for this historic meeting between two teams who don't even play each other in the regular season anymore. Indiana had a great team—Cody Zeller, Christian Watford, Victor Oladipo, and some little white guy like me who shot a better three-point percentage than most people did from the line. They knew they had a shot at the number-one team in America, so like it is for all schools who hosted the Wildcats, it was a momentous occasion. Plus, to call a game in Assembly Hall home court advantage for IU is the understatement of the century. For most road games it was normal for the place to get loud in spurts, but in Indiana the deafening roar was nonstop. All of us just kept saying how badly our ears hurt, and since we couldn't hear each other, we kept saying it over and over. At halftime our ears were ringing in the silence of the locker room.

And just when you thought things couldn't get any louder, Watford hit that game-winning buzzer-beater three-pointer to upset the number-one seed in the nation. The decibel level must have peaked at 150 as the IU fans rushed the floor so quickly that Darius Miller, who fell trying to get to the shot, got trampled by the mob. Our teammate got hurt, our ears hurt, and most importantly, our crew tasted the pain of defeat for the first time. And wow, if that didn't put a fire in our players' guts to fuel a furious run at the title. Kidd Gilchrist absolutely despised when ESPN showed that replay and would get so angry all over again. Christian Watford became our Christian Laettner.

All this emotion and loss-induced suffering was actually a wonderful thing for me to behold, something worth celebrating about my teammates. There is an incredibly important distinction between the negative emotion that stems from "I had a bad game" and *my team lost.* One shows that you're self-centered, not so much in it for the team as you are in it for the name on the back of your jersey. The second shows that you're selfless, that you care more about the team's success than your highlight reel. There were games when Anthony Davis scored under five points. If you're Kobe, you're not okay with that. It means you needed to take sixty-five more shots. AD was content. And that was remarkable for me to witness, to celebrate that talent *and* selflessness in someone else.

For me, that's what made this team special. That's why we were hanging a banner at the end of the year. It was almost like the tournament run had been beautifully scripted, since we got to have our revenge against Indiana and then play against Louisville in the final four. Then in the championship game I got the best gift.

I got to take a vacation from all my self-loathing, from the anxiety of not playing, from fear of failure, and from worrying about whether all my work would pay off. I wasn't thinking about any of that when the buzzer sounded, the confetti started raining down, and Kentucky got its eighth championship. The bench players and I bolted out of our seats, and the ecstasy of celebrating with our teammates took everything else into the background. I will never forget that moment because I was taken completely out of myself into the beautifully free world of delighting in someone else's glory. We jumped up and down on that floor like fools, doing dance moves we had no business doing, completely lost in the bliss of a little kid who just witnessed his favorite team winning it all. There was no time for self-consciousness.

Maybe that helps explain the euphoric reaction that followed from the fans after we cut down the nets. Back at our hotel, which overlooked Bourbon Street, the Big Blue Nation filled the street under our balconies as we made it rain beads for an hour like we were some kind of kings offering valuable relics from our treasury.

When we landed back in Lexington the following day, thousands of people were lined up to greet us at the airport. The royal welcome continued. As we made the twenty-five-minute bus ride, there were people everywhere standing outside and waving—people on their front porches; people standing outside their businesses; people standing in the streets. And for those who didn't live in Lexington, there was a helicopter taking aerial video to make sure avid fans didn't have to miss the exciting footage of our bus driving us home. If there was anyone left in Kentucky, they were waiting at Rupp. The bus literally drove into the arena, where we climbed out one by one to be properly introduced and celebrated by a crowd of twenty-four thousand people. I have never seen Rupp Arena get that loud.

Do you get the sense that this whole experience was over the top? I mean, are these people completely insane? Maybe. Fans may be nuts, but they too were teaching me a great deal about the answer to my problem. In an arena full of twenty-four thousand people I was the only one thinking about myself. My year had been plagued by self-focus: my work ethic, my playing time, my performance, my being hurt by people's comments, my undiscovered talent, my silent suffering. Had I continued to look only at myself, I never would have seen all the good things happening *outside* of me. My identity had been completely wrapped up in my name on the back of a jersey, and my family didn't raise me that way. They raised me to believe that my identity as a child of God was far more important than anything else. And while I claimed to worship Jesus, looking back I was far too busy with my quest to have people worship me. C. S. Lewis writes, "True humility is not thinking less of yourself, but thinking of yourself less."[1]

---

[1] C.S Lewis, *Mere Christianity (New York City, New York, MacMillan Pub. Co., 1952) 123*

I thought I was being humble by acknowledging that I lacked talent, tearing myself down, or making less of myself if I got a compliment. Ironically, I had become as prideful as possible, and while claiming to follow God, I had forgotten about Him. Luckily, I learned a great deal about selflessness and faith from the unlikeliest of sources: twenty-four thousand screaming fans. The members of the Big Blue Nation were experts on worship. They bow before their television sets in prayer during close games. They raise their hands in adoration during wild plays. They jump up and down like fools after an alley-oop. They cry when the season ends in defeat. And they completely lose themselves when a championship is secured. What's funny is that I grew up in church, which is meant to have the corner on worship. But men often feel weird about their posture at church. No one sits in the front row, and everyone's careful to clap on beat, if at all. If a wife asked her husband, "Honey, why didn't you raise your hands during that song?" he might reply, "Well, I don't know what people will think of me if I do that. They might wonder if I really love God or if I'm just doing it for show … and I wouldn't want to do it with the wrong motive."

This would never happen at a basketball game. This same man would pay big bucks to get into the front row. He would scream his head off and jump around like a fool, raise his hands at every swished three-pointer, and sing his heart out at the national anthem and "My Old Kentucky Home." Not once would he think, *If I raise my hands to put on three goggles in celebration of this Wiltjer trey, what if people look at me and wonder if I really love Kentucky or if I'm am just doing it for show?*

It's a humorous scenario because the fan would be so into the game that he would be entirely unconscious, completely lost in the ecstasy of giving himself to something bigger than himself. *He's not concerned with his appearance or his problems because both are swallowed by his love for the team.* And thus, it becomes easy to see why so many men have traded worship on Sunday aimed at a God they can't see for worship on SportsCenter they can watch twenty-four hours a day.

I sent a tweet out the day after winning the championship that read: "I've never seen so many people so passionate about something. I can only think this is what heaven will be like, times a million, praising God!"

Yes, I knew I would get the sacrilegious comments, but looking back, I think there was a hint of truth to it that I didn't really understand at the time. Obviously, heaven will be much greater than a celebration inside Rupp Arena, but what I saw that day had to have been a glimpse at the heart of what heaven consists of. And that heart is simply a bunch of souls who are not concerned with their appearance or problems because both are swallowed by their love for God. I know personally that it would be a lot easier to worship God in an authentic way if I was so engrossed in His glory that I couldn't possibly be concerned with my own problems or appearance.

This idea also helped me understand how the professionals can have it all and yet still not be content. I am particularly intrigued by an interview that aired on *60 Minutes* with Tom Brady.

"I'm making more money now than I ever thought I'd make playing football. Why do I have three Super Bowl rings and still think there is something greater out there for me? Maybe a lot of people would say, 'Hey, man, this is what it is. I reached my goal, my dream, my life … Me, I think it's gotta be more than this.'"

After a brief pause, the interviewer asks him a simple question. "What do you think it is?"

Tom, in a childlike way, responds back, "I wish I knew ... I wish I knew."

That might not make sense to a lot of people since Tom has basically fully arrived at every aspect of the American dream. He's playing the sport he loves and has three Super Bowl rings, all the money he could want, and the icing on the cake, a supermodel wife. Something more, Tom? What else is there?

I believe that he is on to something. C. S. Lewis would agree. "If we find ourselves with a desire that nothing in this world can satisfy, the most probable explanation is that we were made for another world."[2]

Poor Tom was looking for the answer in the wrong place. Luckily for me, his quotes were a reminder that I had begun looking in the wrong place. Brady had what I thought I wanted—the ultimate sports success story. And yet, he wasn't content. There was still a desire in him that wasn't satisfied by his accomplishments. I guess when you're on the throne, it's hard to imagine anything above you.

All of this reminded me that I was looking for fulfillment in the wrong places. Success wasn't going to fix me, and playing time wasn't going to quench my deepest desires. Unlike Tom, I claimed to know the answer. But somewhere along the way I stopped living it out. It took me a good year to get outside myself enough to see that the answer was not going to come from getting what I wanted.

---

[2] C.S Lewis, *Mere Christianity (New York City, New York, MacMillan Pub. Co., 1952) 31*

— 13

The Rise of the Phoenix

Hard work beats talent when talent doesn't work hard.
—Tim Notke

During my junior year, I was determined to remember what Tom Brady taught me during his interview. I stopped allowing my heart to obsess over the idea that more playing time would fix my soul. My goal was no longer to make myself look good for the fans and prove something to the world. I just wanted to help my Wildcats who I had loved since I was a kid. And the great irony of my junior year was that in giving up that idol, I was blessed with the opportunity to help my team *and* get some playing time.

Now, forgive me while I highlight a few personal memories from a season that most Kentucky fans are permanently trying to forget. During Calipari's worst year at Kentucky, I experienced some things that I will forever cherish.

Being a junior had its own built-in advantages. As one, you're considered an upperclassman at any university, but at a school where most players leave after a year, being around the program for three years practically gave me coach status. Players took more of an interest in asking for my advice and actually took me seriously. This was definitely a new phenomenon. It seemed like just yesterday John Wall was asking me who the *bleep* I was and the squad wouldn't even guard me during pick-up games. Now players like Alex Poythress and Archie Goodwin and Willie Cauley-Stein were asking me to bestow my wisdom. And in the pick-up games, I actually needed to be guarded. Not only that, but I could make a difference in the blue/white scrimmage.

During the scrimmage that year I played really well, good enough to lead the second team to victory over the projected starters. I had a confidence now that I could play again, and that confidence made all the difference. I had walked through the valley of failure and come out the other side stronger, focused, and ultimately, free. My life was no longer hinging on my success on the court, since I had already had two years to learn that it was okay to screw up, that fear could no longer cripple me. It doesn't matter how much talent you have … fear can kill it all. And now, I was able to use my experience to mentor and set an example for other players.

Coach Cal recognized my performance after the blue/white game, giving me a sort of secondhand compliment through a knock on Ryan Harrow.

"Ryan, Jarrod outplayed you," he said in the locker room. He continued. "Harrow, if you're going to lead this team, you're going to have to be a lot better."

I had been on the other side of that before and knew how it felt. Harrow was experiencing the same crushing pressure that all of Cal's point-guard pedigree experience: the weight of the world riding on their performance.

I had walked through that valley already and had found the cure. Or I suppose I shouldn't give myself too much credit since it was really Kenny Payne who introduced me to the medicine. He came up and talked to me after we got dressed.

"JP, I told you that you could compete on this level."

"Thanks, Coach," I said with a big smile on my face.

"Just keep playing with confidence kid, and Coach is gonna be forced to play you this year."

"Thanks, Coach. Thanks for everything … I won't let you down."

It was short little conversations like this with KP that gave me enough confidence to play the way I was capable of playing. At this point I just needed a shot. And when that shot didn't come during the first two exhibition games when we blew out our opponents, I began to believe again that I would have another year of waiting.

And then came the Maryland game. After two years of stagnant disappointment, I finally got the chance to play in a game that mattered and make a difference as to whether Kentucky won or lost. I got to taste the joy of being recognized, of knowing that Dick Vitale said positive things about me to a national audience.

My family had waited all this time to see me do something for the Cats, and the wait had been worth it. Coach Cal, who had questioned whether I belonged on the team, said to the press, "He was ready for his opportunity, and as a coach, there is nothing that makes me happier. The whole team was hugging him in there. I'm proud of Jarrod. Jarrod's someone who comes every day and does the things that he needs to do. He doesn't try to do more, and that's what he did tonight. He was just outstanding."

"I go back to the word *crazy*," my dad said when being interviewed by the paper. "I looked at my wife and said, 'Did you ever think in your life that you'd see Dick Vitale and Digger Phelps talking about our son on national TV? It just blew our minds."

Mark Turgeon, the head coach of Maryland, was also in a state of shock. I wasn't even in their scouting report at all, so he had no idea who I was. And then in the post-game conference he said, "He was the whole key to the game. He gave them confidence."

The year before I had zero confidence at all. And now it was the gift that I was giving to the team. For most people it's the same: we have to come to the end of ourselves and be reborn before we have anything to offer anyone else. And I got to taste that glorious redemption my junior year.

The glory was different now, though. I knew that it would fade; I had tasted it before. The true best feeling in the world was having fought on the field of battle to help my beloved team to victory. I was helping my team. It was that pure and simple. And it wasn't just my playing time that helped. It was my example. Harrow was my competition, and yet I didn't see him that way. He was a fellow teammate who wanted the same thing I wanted: to win. And when interviewed, he said he saw in me the joy that his game was missing, and it made him aware of what he needed to change.

"Look at him. He's always so excited and just having fun," Harrow said. "If we don't have fun with each other out there, it's going to be bad." (*Courier Journal*)[3]

If you could ask the fans to summarize the 2012 to 2013 Kentucky basketball season in one word, it's unlikely that anyone would use the word fun.

We lost a lot that year. We lost players. Darius Miller, Terrence Jones, Michael Kidd-Gilchrist, Doron Lamb, Anthony Davis, Marquis Teague, and Eloy Vargas all left us.

We lost players not only to graduation or the NBA but also to injury. The great Nerlens Noel fell victim to a torn ACL, and his fall took down a lot of our tournament hopes.

---

[3] Kyle Tucker, *Look Back- Jarrod Polson a Kentucky basketball blue blood,* Courier Journal, Dec 29, 2012

We lost ranking too, just about every week our seeding slipped as we watched our preseason number three slowly chip away until we completely fell out of the top twenty-five.

The year before we lost two games. The whole year. This year we lost to Duke, Notre Dame, Baylor, Louisville, Texas A&M, Alabama, Florida, Tennessee, Arkansas, and Georgia.

And the losing didn't stop there. We lost in the SEC tournament to Vanderbilt. When it feels like all you're doing is losing, it helps to focus on the things you do have, the things you're thankful for. As cheesy and cliché as that sounds, it truly is the times of loss that you can see what really matters and appreciate the small things as very real blessings. Every once in a while we are forced to remember that the destination might not be quite as important as the journey.

One of my blessings during this year of loss was the Tennessee game. It was the game after Nerlens Noel got injured for the rest of the season, and Coach was looking for a spark, to try something different in hopes of finding some much-needed midseason magic.

"Jarrod, you'll be starting at point tomorrow," he said to us the night before the game. I could barely contain my excitement, and I wanted to text everyone I knew with the good news. However, I knew last-minute changes were not rare for Coach, so I stifled my excitement, and I only texted a few friends and my dad.

The game began, and I was on the floor for the tip-off, leading the team at point guard. I never believed in a million years that I would get to start for Kentucky during a regular-season game. And during it I scored my career high in points, which was a great personal accomplishment following my contribution during the Maryland game. The bad news is this memory is soiled by the fact that Tennessee crushed us by thirty points on their home turf.

Another loss. And with another loss, one more opportunity to pause and take note of the things that matter. Fallen comrades matter. Nerlens left a huge hole in his absence, especially defensively. He was our most outstanding player that year, a no-brainer lottery pick in the draft. A guy like that didn't need to play defense every play like his life depended on it. And yet that's exactly what he did. He was a hustle maniac. And his greatest strength is exactly what took him out for the season. He hustled the length of the court to get to a layup that was nearly impossible to contend and blew out his knee on a play that would immortalize him not only as a player of massive talent but also of a massive heart who found quitting on any play an impossibility. He was a center, an explosive big man, but he was also a leader by his example and his passion. And that's why without finishing the season, Noel would still be drafted at the end of the season and join the NBA.

In Nerlen's absence, the losing continued. As the NCAA tournament was creeping closer and closer, it became evident that we were not a shoe-in as we had been the previous four years. We really needed a perfect run in the SEC tournament to give us the best chance at getting in as a bubble team. But the Vanderbilt game turned out to be a nightmare. I tried to go over a screen instead of trailing the guy I was guarding on a play toward the beginning of the game, and he hit a three, so I had to watch most of the game unfold from the bench. They ended up beating us by sixteen points that day, and as a team, the best way to describe us was paralyzed. Coach Cal walked into the locker room, where we waited for him to say something that might give us some direction, some hope, or perhaps a good reaming. He wasn't necessarily known for long post-game speeches, but this is all he said: "Welp, let's get to the bus and see if we made it or not on Sunday."

We arrived home that night and still had a couple days until the selection show. The anxious anticipation is real; we had to wait in agonizing mystery without any clues as to whether we were bound for the NCAA or the NIT. The overwhelming intuition was that we were not going to make it, but there was always that outside chance that meant hoping wasn't completely futile. That's another thing you learn a lot about during times of loss: hope.

I had a mix of anger, sadness, and confusion inside of me that night that I couldn't let go of. I decided I needed to get out of the lodge and get away from the tense cloud floating above it, so I drove home to Wilmore in hopes that a dose of hometown air would solve the woes. And my parents tried to cure it with their positivity.

"C'mon, Jarrod! You've had a great season. Focus on that. Don't worry about what you can't control."

"It's Kentucky! You guys will get in. They've got to think about TV ratings."

"If they'd played you more, you'd be in the tournament for sure!"

"Well, you guys lost Nerlens, so no one will blame you for not making it into the tournament."

"Eat this dipping cheese, and you'll forget all about your problems."

"Let go, and let God."

"Even without Nerlens, you beat Florida a couple weeks ago… so that's gotta be enough to push you in."

"Remember the Maryland game? Just live in that moment for the rest of your life."

"I know, we could watch *Masked Marvel* 1 through 3. Or how 'bout your favorite: *High School Musical*!"

"Jarrod, you've had worse. Just think about the time Grandpa massaged your intestines and the pain nearly killed you."

Despite all of their encouragement, I literally didn't say a word the whole night. I just laid there on the floor in the living room and pushed a rocking chair back and forth over and over, replaying the bad moments of the last game in my head. I don't even know what happened, but I was so engrossed in my Kentucky pity party that I smashed the chair into the window, completely cracking it. Talk about embarrassing. I had been in the worst mood I'd endured in forever, my parents had just spent their night trying to talk away the darkness, and the only sentence I could muster the entire evening was, "Hey, I just broke your window."

Without paying attention to how I got there, basketball had consumed so much of my energy that my destructive thoughts had seeped out through my arms and began wreaking havoc on my parents' furniture. Luckily though, the window was the only casualty before Sunday rolled around and the team met at Coach Cal's to watch the NCAA tournament selection show. We waited until the very last team was called, and that team wasn't Kentucky. After a few seconds of awkward silence, Cal popped into the living room where all the players were sitting and simply said, "Welp, the NIT it is, boys. Ya'll can leave now."

One by one, without a peep, we walked out of his house into the vans on a cold and gloomy night that matched our mood and rode back to the lodge, where we had the chance to sulk about the results. The next day at practice Coach made it clear that the time for feeling sorry for ourselves was over.

"Boys, I think by now you realize that you don't deserve to play in the NCAA tournament. So let's put it behind us. We deserve to be in the NIT. If you don't feel like playing in the NIT, you can leave. You can be done."

Obviously no one dared to walk out of the gym, even if they wanted to. But you could tell that the practices leading up to our first competition *not* in the big dance were not nearly as intense as the ones during the season. It was apparent that the fire was gone, and we were just tired of losing things. Now we had lost our chance to play in the national tournament and would have to lose our pride enough to go out and compete against a school that most of our players had never heard of.

———

We arrived at the small university in Moon Township, Pennsylvania, and the wild folks in the Charles L. Sewall Center made it clear that they had heard of us. When we got there, long before the game started, the high school–sized gym was already at capacity. They were going nuts, and that was understandable, since our arrival brought the chance for their obscure program to knock off a tradition-filled college basketball titan like Kentucky on ESPN. Their fans weren't the only ones fired up. The game began, and before we could blink, the Robert Morris Colonials were up on us ten to nothing. These little defenders of freedom were living up to their name, and we were initially in shock at the atmosphere, the athleticism, and the skill of the Robert Morris players, who we assumed we would come in and walk all over. And then there was the fact that the Colonials had everything to fight for in this match, and our players felt a bit like a defeated samurai who would rather just lower his neck and submit to a quick and painless finish.

Once again, at the end of a long and tumultuous season, we were faced with the prospect of loss, to a team that had no business competing with us on paper. Coach did not like the way the game was headed, and so he started subbing. So once again, with the impending doom actually came great opportunity. When I went in, I refused to play like someone who was already defeated. I was not going to lower my neck in submission no matter what opponent we faced and regardless of the title of the tournament. We were still wearing the jerseys that said "Kentucky" on the front, and I meant to play like that even if no one else felt like it. It was time for me to lead again.

I scored several times in the first half. We started to gain some momentum in this dogfight, where initially we had no fight to offer. But I was not going to quit. I played a career high in minutes that night, and in those thirty-one minutes, I may have played the best in my career. I shot 80 percent from the field and led the team in assists.

Digger Phelps was commentating that night and apparently pointing out that it didn't seem any Wildcats besides me and Archie Goodwin had any fight left in them.

"Polson's gonna get a lot of playing time tonight, 'cause Calipari's looking to play people who are tough."

We were told before the game by the coaches, "All year you play for the name on the front of the jersey. Tonight it's about the name on the back. Will you play with pride in yourself?"

That night I played with pride in myself. I left it all on the court that final game of my junior season, so it didn't even matter what the final score was. I refuse to quote the final score here because it is no indication of who won and who lost. I could stand there at the end of the game while Robert Morris fans rushed the floor and appreciate the joy they had in what they accomplished, while simultaneously appreciating the satisfaction in knowing that I too had done what I set out to accomplish. Contrary to popular belief, sometimes losing can also be winning. I had to learn that the worst season I had been a part of at Kentucky could also be a year ascribed to my memory and the memory of my family as a year of triumph. And while the Big Blue Nation will probably do its best to forget that year and the Robert Morris tragedy that ended it, I will never forget. I will remember the year when I learned what it means to have joy in loss and to give everything you have even though you might not get the results you're dying for. After all, it truly is about the journey, not the destination.

———

My junior year was special not because of my skill or great plays but because of the symbolic victory it brought for the underdog, for the walk-on, for all people everywhere who feel like life is overlooking them. Deep down I think everyone wants to have moments in life when the success or failure of some great enterprise rests on their shoulders and they are able to bear the burden without falling. We all crave some kind of epic responsibility and the courageous fortitude to accomplish what is needed. It's why hero movies are so enticing to our imaginations. If you break down the heroic plots to the skeletons of these stories, it's hard not to chuckle at how silly they are. A small creature called a hobbit with hairy feet saves the world by destroying an evil ring? Or *Guardians of the Galaxy*, where a group of misfit good guys (including a raccoon and a selfless tree man named Groot) needs to defeat a crazed villain named Ronin who has a big hammer.

Despite their ridiculousness, we eat them up—not because the stories make any sense but because we desperately long to be a part of a story in which we have a tangible purpose through which our abilities meet the world's deepest needs. Basketball isn't any great need in the world, but in our culture we're so starving for significance that we'll accept worshiping a guy who hits a three-pointer at the buzzer because it gives us a taste of the glory we're after. We've invented an arsenal of sports and games to give ourselves the feeling of accomplishment and victory on a scale that's not actually forcing us to risk anything.

So just as our favorite stories and movies may be insignificant in and of themselves but hold the incredible power of inspiring symbolism, my journey in basketball means nothing in the grand scheme of the world except that it gave a window into the beautiful imagery of the underdog having his day. It gives hope to us normal mortals in the world who feel defeated by the crazy talented people who always hog the spotlight and woo us with their powers. In the long run it will not be the magnificent powers of man's strength we will be worshiping anyway. There are more powerful and worthy forces we should be pursuing that aren't as flashy but are far more important to the world than the raw talent of Terrence Jones dunks or Kyle Wiltjer three-bombs. And I got a glimpse of those God-given forces during my time at Kentucky. I waited three years for my chance to play and compete on the Division 1 stage, which showed that my skill is not as important as the virtue of *patience*. After falling victim to the mentality that focuses on what *I* deserve, I realized that the selfish wish to be appreciated does not hold a candle to the virtue of *selflessness*, the desire to see those around me get better. Coming into school I believed the only prerequisite for leadership was talent, and after this season it became clear to me that the best way to lead is making a difficult choice to step into a messy situation when others might not be so keen on taking the initiative.

With these lessons learned, I didn't care how many losses we had, what tournament we played in, or what our ranking was going to look like heading into the next season. Nothing could take away the glimpses I had into what really matters in life.

There was one more loss to suffer through at the end of this year, and that was the loss of being able to sleep in and rest after a long and arduous journey. We had to be up early every day after the Robert Morris loss to do twenty suicides in twenty minutes at 6:00 a.m. Coach was trying to see what we were made of and if anyone would break down and quit. His threat was that if anyone was late or didn't show up to these running sessions, he would be kicked off the team. I showed up every day, on time, and no amount of aerobic sprinting torture was going to break me. They were physically miserable, and they certainly took a lot out of me. But hey, sometimes losing is winning.

— 14

Ethiopian Adventure

This was the driving force in His life. Jesus knew how special all people were. He knew they were created in God's image. He knew they had eternity marked in their hearts.
—Tom Davis, Author of Red Letters

Up to this point we've been exploring the journey of my basketball career, with its ups and downs. If you're a sports fan, I assume you've realized as I have that the greatest thing about the sport you love isn't actually the game itself. If you've played sports, you don't look back on your years as an athlete and delight simply in how much fun the competition was, but you get a dose of pleasant nostalgia when you remember the lessons you learned, the friends you made, and the relationship you had with the coach who made a difference.

The thing that makes sports worth our while, like all good entertainment, is that it harnesses the power of story. The commentators for *Sunday Night Football* understand this, and they talk about not just records and statistics for each team but about the backstory of the players, the drama laden in the history of the team's competitions, or the personal difficulties the coach has overcome in his life. And even if you're watching a game and you know nothing about any of the players, the coaches, or how many yards you need for a first down, you can still get caught up in the story that every game has to tell—the story of the underdog.

By definition, to root for the underdog is an act of faith. You choose to ignore the black-and-white statistics on paper saying one team has a better record, more talented players, and home-court advantage. You choose to believe that there are unseen forces of the heart or of seemingly miraculous circumstances that can propel a team to victory when they didn't have the supposed credentials to pull it off. The story of the underdog demands faith, and that's probably why it will never go away.

To me, faith is one of the most difficult but also the most rewarding elements in this life. After my junior year, which brought the chance to live out my dream of *playing* for Kentucky, I had tasted everything that I had wished to experience as a kid. And yet, like Tom Brady, I could sense that there were things out there that I had not completely figured out or experienced. So if I may, allow me to take you on an adventure that has more to do with my journey of faith than it does with my basketball career.

See, I was raised in a Christian home. A family's religion may sound like something passed down from generation to generation, another factor of your identity you're born into that has as little to do with choice as the color of your eyes. It's like when you go to give blood, you answer all kinds of questions about things that define you whether you chose them or not.

"Blood type?"

"A positive."

"Race?"

"Caucasian."

"Date of birth?"

"February 10, 1978."

"Sexual orientation?"

"Huh?"

"Religious background?"

"Christian."

"That answers the previous question."

The problem is that your religion and your faith are completely different things. You can be a Christian by birth, as in your parents claim that affiliation, and yet you personally have no real faith. Conversely, you can claim no religious affiliation whatsoever and have remarkable faith.

My parents are examples of both. My dad came from a family who professed to believe in God but had no serious connection with any organized religion. My mom grew up in Wilmore and had extremely devout Christian parents who were heavily involved in Asbury Seminary. And ironically, my dad is the figure in our household who claims that even before he knew anything about theology or doctrine, he had unshakeable faith in Christ. It was my mother, who could play and sing "O Holy Night" on the piano at the national prayer breakfast from the age of two, who struggled mightily with doubt. She was always very honest about her internal emotional battles with the unconditional love of God. There's an old joke that says some Christians who fear they are constantly falling out of God's good graces are like the little girl holding the flower and pulling petals off one by one, saying, "He loves me … he loves me not." Perhaps my mother's struggle was less about faith in God and more about whether He had faith in her. But for all her doubting and endless verbal confessions, she painted a vivid picture of our endless need of divine forgiveness.

I say this to give you a little background on the spiritual thermometer in which I grew up. I was raised in as Christian a home as there ever has been. But as I said, your faith is not something you inherit genetically from your father. It seems that though I was very connected to the Christian religion, I had my own questions and my own doubts. I was never a true prodigal son, tempted by the forbidden fruits of the world so much that I wanted to live my high school years in pursuit of sex, drugs, and rock and roll. We have Christian rock and roll now so that temptation should be silenced. As for sex, there would be all of that we can handle when we got married.

If I were to run away from my parents' religion, it wasn't going to be a dramatic show of outward rebellion. My struggle was going to be an internal one, a questioning of the reality behind the things that were preached from the pulpit or read from the Bible I knew since I was young. If you grew up in the church, went to vacation Bible school when your friend invited you, or even watched *Veggie Tales* as a kid, you have probably been struck by the peculiar nature of the stories you learned about from the Holy Scriptures.

One of the first songs you learn: "Jesus loves me, this I know, for the Bible tells me so ..."

One of the first stories you learn: Noah's ark. When you're little this story is cool because it's every kid's dream: God tells you to build a giant boat and rewards you with your own personal zoo. And then as you get older, you realize that the real point of the story is a cataclysmic flood of judgment meant to kill everyone on the planet.

The yin and the yang of God's love and the simultaneous suffering of this world have been the great intellectual barrier for as long as humans have tried to make sense of any theology or religion. I would be lying to you if I said that I've never questioned God's existence. Growing up in a Christian home doesn't make that question disappear. In fact, I would argue that it probably makes the question even more difficult. What I mean is, believing the right things doesn't mean that life is going to be perfect. It doesn't mean your circumstances will magically work out like you hope. My own home life was an example of that. My parents could be described as people of perfect faith. And yet, despite that, they did not have a picture-perfect family in the beginning. I was born within a year of my parents' marriage, what some might call an accident, and as I grew up, I got to know my two older brothers— brothers born during my mother's first marriage. I grew up with two half-brothers and two full sisters. It was great, but it was a blended family that carried with it an expected level of brokenness. It's not that my dad drank to escape the chaos of a family with five kids or that my half-brothers abused me. In fact, the messiness was that my brothers left me every weekend to play house with my sisters when I wanted to be shooting hoops.

No great amount of suffering there, especially in the grand scheme of planet earth's atrocities. My physical pain or mild depressions are small potatoes for a divine being of my own imagination, let alone the one found in the Bible. I grew up learning about the God who created billions of galaxies, who made the mountains, who made the woman, who parted the Red Sea, who knocked down the walls of Jericho, who saved Daniel from the lions, who gave David the strength to kill Goliath, who came to earth as a baby, who healed all sorts of diseases, who humbled the arrogant religious leaders, and who raised Jesus from the dead.

Is curing my little depressions or keeping my brothers around for two weeks straight too much to ask from a God with such a fantastic history of miracles? I highly doubt my desires were above His power level. And yet, it seemed to me that maybe He wasn't really in the miracle business during the twenty-first century. So while I grew up a Christian, I didn't really have much real faith. Faith is the ability to see God working in the world, but I had never seen God work in a dramatic way like the stories from the Bible. And that didn't make a lot of sense, to say that we believed in the

God of the Bible and in Jesus without any evidence that He existed in the world today. Historically speaking, He could walk on water, but He had not miraculously showed up and fixed any problems that I could see. My problems are humorous illustrations. It doesn't get funny when we start thinking about the tragedies of global proportions. I don't know why around twenty-one thousand people (mostly children) die every day from starvation. I don't know why we've lost so many people from cancer and it doesn't feel like we're any closer to a cure. I don't know why there are still twenty to thirty million people in slavery because of human trafficking. I don't know why hundreds and hundreds have been beheaded by ISIS.

It is difficult to swallow the reality of the harshness of this world. And when confronted with statistics like these, it feels like singing, "Jesus loves me, this I know" on Sundays is more of an escapist's distraction than it is an answer to any of these problems.

Again, I would be lying if I said I have never asked, "Where is the all-powerful, good, loving God in the midst of our world's suffering?"

My grandpa took me to see a documentary called *Expelled* where Ben Stein attempts to defend the academic integrity of intelligent design, a theory proposing that the complexity and "fine tuning" required for earth to support life is evidence of a creator. In a nutshell, it's really intelligent people trying to *prove* that God exists. Toward the end of the film, Ben interviews Richard Dawkins, who is a famous critic of religion and outspoken atheist whose most famous work is titled *The God Delusion*, which pretty well explains his position.

Ben struggles to get him to admit even the slightest possibility that God might actually exist, so he settles for Richard entertaining an imaginary scenario.

"Let's say you die, and you find out that God is real. So you meet Him, face-to-face. What would you say?" Ben asked. Dawkins pauses, thinks for a moment, trying to humor him with an answer to a question he is confident will never become a reality.

"I would ask God," he replies, "*why did you take such pains to hide Yourself?*"

This is the great question that I think every honest person has to wrestle with. Why does it feel like God is hiding from us? I had the same feeling since God had never revealed Himself to me in any dramatic or miraculous way like writing in the clouds or speaking to me out of a burning bush. At this point in my life, I began to wonder if I had been looking in the wrong places.

I had pursued my dreams, had actually gotten the opportunity to play basketball for the University of Kentucky. I was twenty-one years old and had accomplished the majority of my bucket list. Now what?

During the summer the UK athletic department began an initiative to take eight to ten athletes on a weeklong service trip to Africa. This year, the team would head to Ethiopia, and I was informed that I was chosen to go that year. I didn't hesitate to say yes, since I had always wanted to go to Africa and had never had the opportunity to go to a third-world country. Under my current life circumstances, I knew that this trip would be really good for me, even though I had no idea what to expect. Others who returned from similar trips would always say things like, "My perspective has totally changed on life," or other really profound statements that made you feel like you had to take the plunge. I figured I probably needed to be careful looking for too much life change, since I was pretty much as on top of the world as I'd ever be. However, I still had this nagging feeling that God was hiding somewhere. And I had a sneaking suspicion that I might gain some eyes to see with a fresh perspective on things. With all the hype that people place on trips like these, I was definitely expecting a divine lightning bolt of miraculous proportions. What I got was more of a quiet, subtle, baby-in-a-manger type of surprise. I would like to give you a few snapshots of my trip. I don't want to show you the land, the massive political problems, or a portrait of the illnesses that ravage so many. I would like to show you a few portraits of some special individuals who I will never forget.

On our third day in Ethiopia, we met a woman who was a single mom plagued with a variety of illnesses. She was trying to survive and make ends meet to provide sustenance for her kids by running her own food booth out on the strip. We wanted to help her out, so we gave her bread. Nothing too heroic, but we felt like the small gesture could go a long way. It felt good to know that her kids wouldn't have to worry that day about where their next meal would come from. A few hours later we were in a different place and were surprised to see the same woman again. She had not stayed home to feast with her children but was out handing away the same bread to her hungry friends in the community.

We met another woman who was infected with HIV, which in our world is all people would need to define her. However, this person was not allowing her life to be characterized solely by the disease she had. She was the hospitality queen, consistently bringing in travelers from different villages even though she could barely afford to. She used her opportunities with different people as a platform to share the gospel. For her efforts, she took constant ridicule from her sons, who thought her beliefs were absurd. And yet, she still loved them and provided for them unconditionally. She had every reason to quit, but she didn't.

Another snapshot came through our interaction with the young translators who we got to spend a lot of time with. These two young men had known the meaning of suffering. One was an orphan and the other a street kid, and both had their stories to tell. The most poignant was when they were ten years old and sent up into the mountains on their own because of a "street cleaning." They witnessed their friend being killed and eaten by a hyena in those mountains. In our understanding these are the most difficult tragedies to swallow because they are seemingly random, and you can't point to man's selfishness as the cause of the loss. Growing up in America some kids never fully recover from the loss of their dog. In Ethiopia these two boys had to mourn the fact that a wild dog had killed their best friend. Despite cause for bitterness, however, these two were the most grateful and joy-filled humans I have ever had the privilege to meet.

The next crew I must introduce you to were the youth impact leaders at the church we went to. These guys were extremely intelligent and had made it in terms of their education and potential for successful occupations in nicer areas of Ethiopia or even in America. They had a chance to run away from the difficulty of their homes and never look back, chasing a dream of money and comfort. But they didn't leave. Instead, they chose to be pastors in one of the poorest, most populated villages called Korah, where one hundred thousand people live inside of a square mile of land.

One final snapshot, and I will conclude my tour. We entered into a tiny home in one of the villages to deliver some food to another woman. She couldn't accept the food herself, not because she was too prideful or anything but because this woman had no feet and no fingers. A victim of leprosy, this woman had been lying in bed for eighteen years. The mere sight of her circumstances was appalling, let alone having to live in her situation for that amount of time. We wanted to pray for her, and the compassion welling up inside of us would have been happy for a divine miracle to rid this woman of her suffering. I placed my hand on her head as we started to pray, and the interpreters told me she was pleading for me to take my hand off. Apparently, she didn't want me to get sick. This woman had survived unspeakable horror for the majority of her life and she was worried about *me*? Then as we visited with her, there was one phrase that she kept repeating over and over again. Understanding her was really difficult, but with the interpreters' help, we realized what she was chanting like a broken record.

"God bless you. God bless you. God bless you."

In this moment I realized that my hide-and-seek game with God was coming to an end. I remember feeling unbelievably sorry for this woman and her trial with leprosy. Her body was so cruelly marred that I recall the initial difficulty in recognizing whether or not she was human at all. That's how badly this disease had impacted her life. Most people would take one look at her and jerk their eyes away, wondering how someone could be so robbed of their humanity. And yet, in this jar of clay, this hollow casing of a woman with no fingers or toes, was a selfless spirit who cared about us. She was so thankful that we came to visit her and could do nothing except wish a blessing over our lives. God bless *us*? The divine had clearly set up shop in this remarkable shell of humanity, and my suspicions were proved true. She was not human. She was something far better.

I learned on this trip that I was looking for God in the wrong places. I said I was looking for God most of my life, but it turns out I was really looking for something He could give me. The Bible says that you can see Jesus in "the least of these," which means that you can witness the presence of God when you care for people that the rest of the world overlooks. That's exactly what happened to me in Ethiopia. It's not that God has taken great pains to hide Himself but that we have taken great pains to avoid needing Him.

Sometimes, especially in America, it's hard to see God or feel His presence because by worldly standards, we don't really *need* Him. We can wake up and go a full day without even thinking about Him or giving Him credit for anything. When I went to Ethiopia, I got to meet people who truly walked with God as their shepherd. I was a Christian before I went to Ethiopia, but my friends their taught me about true *faith*. I believe in Jesus 100 percent and not because my parents raised me to or because everything in my life is some kind of joyful fantasy. *I believe in God because I have witnessed people with nothing who possess souls that have everything.* And now I look at the dilemma of suffering in a completely different light. I used to think the biggest miracles I could imagine were ones where God fixes the terrible circumstances and saves the day in some dramatic way. Now I believe that the greatest miracles happen when people stay in their difficulty but have changed hearts and renewed perspectives. I believe in God simply because I cannot accept that the woman living with leprosy was living through her own strength. She was sustained by the love that people gave and the love that she gave away, and she probably lived a more satisfying life in those eighteen years with no arms or legs than we experience in a lifetime of chasing the world's most enticing pleasures. I believe in God because of the woman with HIV, who sacrificed her entire life for the sake of the gospel, even to her own children's disapproval. I don't believe her life would be possible without God's presence living inside of her. I believe in God because I hear crazy stories of Muslims seeing Jesus in their dreams, only to wake up and give their lives to Christ. I believe in God because of the things that I have seen or perhaps more importantly, because of the things I *can't* see. Christians may spend a lot of time trying to prove God exists because it beefs up the argument for the accuracy of their religion. The ironic thing is that if we could systematically remove all doubt that God is real, there wouldn't be any need for faith. And faith, after all, is a beautiful thing. It finds great delight in the things that we cannot see or prove.

I have faith in God for reasons that most people *don't* choose to believe in Him. When you really observe the Bible, it is flat-out crazy. And there are some things it is impossible to make complete sense out of. The God we worship became a baby from an unassuming woman who had never had sex. Then God became a carpenter for thirty years and did a three-year stint of ministry while performing some outrageous miracles and saying some pretty controversial stuff. And then to top it off, He was executed on a cross because of a bunch of jealous Jewish religious leaders who didn't like His claims. However, He miraculously appeared again three days later, making an appearance to around five hundred people, and then floated back to heaven. Since then His followers have been waiting two thousand years for His valiant return. Is this a wild story or what? And this is just a small piece of the New Testament I am paraphrasing here. Some of you reading may be thinking, *Yup, and that's why religion is nuts. And you expect me to believe these things happen.* But for me this actually draws me closer to the truth of Jesus because it is far too outlandish to be made up. If I were trying to make up a religion, or trying to get people to obey me and follow my teachings, I wouldn't make up a story like that. In fact, the whole thing seems so crazy that it's almost impossible to make up a story as beautifully complex as the Bible. And though there are things that make no sense logically, that's exactly why I believe.

I have experienced the great things this world has to offer. I have seen pleasure, power, and fame. I have been along for the crazy miracle story that brought me to Kentucky. I have seen God orchestrate a journey of a little boy from Wilmore, Kentucky, who was about to give up on basketball after high school and then ended up playing for the most prestigious basketball university in the country, which just so happened to be his dream school. And I also discovered that my most outlandish dream couldn't actually satisfy me in any conclusive way. I have learned about the thing that Tom Brady was missing. He was focused on the things that he could gain and the things that he could see. The truth is, *life is most satisfying when you're focused on what you can give.* Now I know why people come back changed after their big mission trips and why they can't wait to go back to countries that might be characterized by poverty, dirtiness, and the despair of suffering. These people discover what it means to love someone as much as you love yourself. In my one week in Ethiopia, I didn't care about myself too much. Seeing the poverty allowed our group to throw away our selfishness and honestly care about people who were less fortunate than us, materially speaking. There is something divine about the feeling you get when you genuinely care for and help another person. There is honestly no other feeling like it. Not even winning a national championship.

In my search to find God, I had to realize that He was never really hiding in the first place. The book of 1 John says, "No one has ever seen God, but if we love one another, God abides in us" (4:12). God is everywhere on this planet, not just in Ethiopia. He's in America too, but unfortunately we often become more obsessed with accumulating things we can see to make us happy. I thought I could go out into the world and teach people about Christianity, and I came home with the realization of who it was that really needed help. As my Ethiopian friend Abraham said the first time he came to visit this country, "I feel sorry for *you guys.* You have so many distractions that it must be so hard to focus on things that really matter."

My impoverished Ethiopian friend who had never cut the nets down after making it to the final four, or won any championship rings, felt sorry for *me*. Of course, he had the most vibrant faith I could possibly imagine. He is from a country that actually has the right to ask where God is in the midst of suffering, and yet he never accuses God of hiding. He sees God every day with crystal clarity. Abraham is right; I should envy him. For all the blessings God has given me during my life, I am beginning to understand which type is more satisfying.

I don't know where you are in your walk of life as you sit and read these pages. You may be a person of strong faith, someone who is still searching, or someone who doesn't even believe in a god at all. What I do know is that we all have different stories, different happenings in our life that affect us in real ways. I was talking to God one night about my story, my testimony, and how it really wasn't all that inspiring, at least in my mind. No one wants to hear a testimony about a kid who grew up in a nice family and has always been a Christian. That was my thinking for as long as I can remember. I'm very careful about telling other people when I think God has spoken to me, but this is one of the only times I know that what I heard in my heart was from God Himself. As I was telling Him my doubts and insecurities about my rather unexciting story, He simply said this: "Your testimony is not about yourself; it is about Me."

I thought about it for a while, and I began to realize the weight of this revelation. Sometimes I think Christians, including myself, get so caught up in our "the world revolves around me" mind-set that we begin to think our walk with Christ is all about ourselves as well. We try to witness to other people by selling them on the things they can obtain when they decide to follow Jesus. We talk about our change of identity, the freedom we have in Christ, the many blessings that will come after repentance, a life of joy, and a peace beyond all understanding. And please don't get me wrong—all of these are wonderful things that God delights in giving us. But I think we are missing out on the most important aspect of being a Christian. It is the greatest commandment in the Bible. "Love the Lord your God with all of your heart and with all of your soul and with all of your mind" (Mark 12:30). We spend so much time thinking and talking about our identity and the things we receive through Jesus that we sometimes forget our ultimate task, to give glory to our Creator. If I had to sell the idea of being a Christian, I would tell someone that the best part is being able to worship the God who knows everything about us, the God who wove us together, the God who chose us to be His children, who loves us unconditionally. We get to have a relationship with the one who invented taste buds, the intricate details of a human body, the chill bumps you get when listening to your favorite song, and the entire universe. The glory of God is unimaginable, something that doesn't even compare to anything we could experience on this earth. Our problem is that we are too easy to please, and we take whatever pleasures we can get in this life, without recognizing the ultimate pleasure of spending eternity in the presence of God. God doesn't disallow seemingly exciting sins because He doesn't want us to have fun but because He has something much greater waiting for us that will make the enticing pleasures of this world seem like filthy rags. Again, I don't know where you find yourself at this exact moment, but I can promise you that giving your life to Jesus is the only way to true fulfillment. It may not make your life look like a fairy tale, and you may not experience as much worldly fun, but you will have the ultimate privilege of bringing glory to the God who not only breathed you into existence but who is also desperately waiting on you to run to Him.

— 15

The Last Hurrah

Do nothing out of selfish ambition or vain conceit, but in humility consider others better than yourselves.
—*Philippians 2:3 NIV*

As the summer came to a close and I was gearing up for my glorious return as a spiritually enlightened senior, I received a very confusing text on my phone from one of the team managers.

"Which one do you want?"

There was a list of about ten different numbers, none of which were mine. I expressed my curiosity.

"What do you mean, which number do I want?"

I had been number five during the first three years at UK. In fact, I had worn the mighty cinco as long as I could remember, and my childhood photos with giant glasses were historically paired with a jersey sporting the number five.

"Here's the deal. Andrew Harrison is going to be number five this year, so we need you to choose a different one."

Instantly I had a flashback to a conversation I had with my dad a few months earlier. "If the Harrison twins commit to Kentucky, you can kiss your number good-bye."

"Nah, they wouldn't do that to me," I answered, not taking his comment seriously.

"You wait and see, but if he comes, he's gonna want that number." Flash forward a couple months, and my dad's prophecy was fulfilled.

Immediately a variety of feelings began to boil up inside of me. As the confusion wore off, anger took its place. First of all, this conversation was taking place through text message, between me and a manager. Common decency informs most people's consciences that there are certain things you do not communicate through text. You should not initiate a major relationship status change through texting. You would never propose to the woman of your dreams with a text, and when you discover she's not the woman of your dreams, you don't break up with her through a text. The number five and I had endured a pretty lengthy love affair, and it seemed like I was being broken up with over a text message. Entitlement immediately washed over me, as I thought to myself, *I'm a senior who has worked my butt off for three years. Why should I give up my number to someone who hasn't even set foot on this campus as a teammate, let alone played a game for Kentucky?*

I didn't know what to say. My friends and family did. People were not happy. My sister Ashley was with me at the time, and I knew I could honor her reaction because she might be no expert in basketball, but I have tremendous respect for her spiritual maturity and wisdom … and her ability to take the deep emotional paradox and put it into layman's terms.

"That's a bunch of garbage! I can't believe they would do that to you," she said.

"It's fine. That's just the way it is," I replied with as much optimism as I could muster.

"That's not the way it is. You deserve that number. You were the only one who even tried last year."

"It's a number. Just forget about it." I ended the conversation abruptly, trying to hide the anger that was inside.

I didn't expect Ashley to understand the hopeless broken heart that a sports' wound can inflict, but the fact that she felt so strongly made me wonder if I should just take this lying down. Ashley was there to sympathize with me emotionally, which was the first thing I needed. My dad was a different story. Although he had called the whole thing and could have celebrated his moment to say, "I told you so," he was ready to go to bat for his son whether or not I asked him to and whether or not it would do any good. He called Orlando Antigua, an assistant coach, and politely but bluntly asked how something like this could happen. My dad closed the conversation by saying, "There are going to be some very upset Kentucky fans."

I wasn't too happy either, but I harnessed my anger instead of saying or doing something I would regret. I could have put up a fight and try to bring the whole thing into the spotlight and focus on the injustice I was feeling. Or I could have said something like a guy did on his Twitter account, who was blunt but not polite

There was the temptation to let bitterness and hatred be the foundation of my opinion of my new teammate even before I shook his hand. I could have mentally decided to carry that grudge with me all year, never really given him a chance, and harnessed that negative energy to make myself practice harder and try to show him who was boss.

But rising up against all these feelings of anger and entitlement was a sudden flashback. I had been to a country where I saw a kid drinking dirty water out of a river with a balloon. And he didn't complain one bit about not having a Brita or a glass of ice or that his water was not infused with electrolytes. Here I was, back in

America, feeling sorry for myself after experiencing the horrific pinnacle of human suffering because I had to switch the number on my jersey. Oh, the inhumanity.

Rather than choosing bitterness, I chose something that many probably perceived as weak. I decided to risk the pending embarrassment and internal disappointment by giving up my number to an incoming freshman without making a big stink about it. And instead of focusing on how much I deserved it, I began to replace that feeling with gratitude for the journey I had been on. I remembered that just a couple years earlier, I wasn't even going to play college basketball. I remembered that I had been given the unbelievable privilege of wearing the Kentucky jersey as a walk-on. I remembered that I was incredibly blessed to make the jump to a scholarship player and had my college career paid for. I remembered that I was lucky to have ever called the number five on a blue jersey mine in the first place.

And because of the choice I made not to harbor any hatred, my year wasn't ruined by bitterness, and I experienced some surprises that I wouldn't have felt otherwise. The first one was this beautiful truth: you can forgive someone, but that forgiveness doesn't mean there aren't still consequences for his actions. The first consequence Andrew received was during the Big Blue Madness Scrimmage. I'm not really a revenge seeker or someone who likes to force three-point attempts when they're not there. But on one play Andrew was facing me up just inside the half-court line as I brought the ball up the court. I couldn't resist. I made a move and quickly changed directions with a cross-over, then launched a deep three-pointer right over Andrew's fully extended hand, which was right in my face.

Buckets. Right in front of the Big Blue Nation, for all to see, the old number five had just put on a clinic for the freshman number five. I didn't say anything. And I didn't need to. The pleasure it gave my family and friends was enough.

But like I said, there was never really any animosity between us because I had chosen to let it go. And good thing, too, because here's what makes the story even more ironic: it turns out that Andrew didn't even know he stole my number. I never said anything to him about it, and he wasn't even told that his request for number five meant that someone else had to give it up. In fact, since this was pretty much a brand new team, they didn't know what number the little walk-on had been the year before.

Toward the end of the season, my high school decided to have a jersey retirement ceremony on my behalf. So in my beloved West Jessamine gym, in front of my community, friends, family, the entire UK team, and Coach Cal, I received the honor of having my high school and college jerseys immortalized behind a glass frame. And both jerseys bore the number five.

You could sense a bit of confusion looming above the heads of the new Kentucky players, who had just watched me play for nearly an entire season wearing the number three. Staring at my jerseys, they raised eyebrows and looked back and forth at each other as the realization sank in. Slowly, the truth was dawning on them as various people were droning on and on about my accomplishments as a player. It was a sacred moment for my family and probably a painful one for Andrew Harrison. Julius Randle looked up at the Kentucky jersey, which read, "Polson ... 5" then looked at Andrew, then back at the jersey, and back at Andrew. Randle then elbowed Harrison in the side.

Of course, for Andrew there could have been no real guilt. The elbow to the ribs can't really be delivered to any one person. It wasn't Andrew's fault, because he didn't know he was forcing another player to give up his number. The manager who texted me doesn't deserve the elbow, because he was just the messenger in the scenario. I could have blamed one of the coaches, but I didn't do the detective work it would've taken to figure out who initially agreed to the condition. I couldn't wish the elbow on the UK basketball program, which is for good reason geared to place highest priority on players with the most amount of raw talent. I knew what I was signing up for when I came into the program as a freshman. In any case, the whole debacle ended up being a simple miscommunication, and I knew that no one involved had any malice in their hearts towards the situation.

I grew to like the number three, which I initially chose because of its reflection of the Holy Trinity (yes, I just played the Christian card), whose help I was going to need to beg for if I was going to get any playing time over our new recruits. And maybe I was blessed by its symbolic power of divine unity because the number did end up having a bit of prophetic wisdom. By the end of the season, though I wouldn't be remembered as a player with big minutes, I did lead the team in a certain percentage: threes. That's an accomplishment I never would have believed I could have had my name next to in the record books, and it probably wouldn't have happened if I chose to go to war against my teammate.

Another awesome surprise that animosity would have robbed me of was the marvelous irony that Andrew and I actually became friends. He's never been to my house for Christmas, but over the season we talked a great deal about running the point, and I was able to give him a lot of advice about playing under Coach Cal. I liked Andrew, and making a choice to forever label him my enemy would never have allowed the freedom of this glorious possibility.

There was another circumstance to allow me to take my mind off of this little drama at the beginning of the year. This was simply that the basketball blues of yesteryear were blowing away, as the incoming class of 2013 was a fresh wind of magnificent hype. Every Cal reload was steeped with anticipation, but this year brought with it a phenomenon I had never witnessed before. Maybe it was just that people were so excited to put the year before it out of memory, and the "forty and zero" talk that spread like wildfire through Lexington was a simple way to drink away the lingering pain. We hadn't played a game or even had a scrimmage, but fans were already making claims about this team going down in history as the best college basketball squad ever assembled.

The external buzz being made by the Harrison twins, Julius Randle, James Young, Marcus Lee, and Dakari Johnson arriving on the scene as reinforcements gave the Bluegrass state a way to rekindle their hope. There were six McDonald's All-Americans coming, as well as two phenomenal in-state players named Dominique Hawkins and Derek Willis, who were both very underrated coming out of high school. Another year brought another round of outrageous talent, which helped our team start to build back some of the swagger we had lost. There was definitely a different feel of excitement with this team with every practice and workout. In the weight room, with Drake instilling wisdom in us through the speakers, we would do our last set of planks for the day and start to dance to the music as emotions about the upcoming season got us all pumped up. Even Coach Rock got into the dancing a little bit, but only when Gucci came on. Pick-up games would end with a James Young three ball or an emphatic rim rattler by Randle, and we would all just look around at each other and smile. Once again, we were tasting the immediate gratification of an entire team super-saturated with Olympic talent. But the question wasn't how much talent we had ... obviously that wasn't the only factor in winning a championship. The question was, were we going to work our tails off and become a cohesive force of domination rather than a bunch of rock stars eager to get their names in the lottery?

As far as the actual season itself went, it sort of mirrored my regression and progression as a player. We were preseason ranked number 1, with all the talk about an undefeated season, and yet we needed to go through some trials and go backward before we could go forward. Personally, I was set to be a solid role player coming off of the bench, and during the second exhibition game that season, I actually had the opportunity to start at point guard because Andrew was out with an injury. We looked decent in those two exhibitions, but that's because players could pretty much do whatever they wanted and score. Defensively and athletically the opposing teams couldn't compete with the size, strength, speed, and versatility that our team had going for it. But things would get tougher, for the team and for me individually.

By the third game of the season, I had somehow found myself out of the rotation, and I resorted back to my original days, riding the bench. We were in for a real test of manhood, slated to play Michigan State, who was ranked right behind us at number two in the nation. This was an awesome atmosphere, about what you would expect during tournament time. Unfortunately I watched the whole thing unfold from my seat, witnessing our chance at forty and zero go down the drain. But this was a good team we lost to, by far the best competition we had faced in the few games we had played as a team. Nobody was giving up championship dreams because of an early season wakeup call at the hands of Tom Izzo. The main thing you want to see after a loss like that one is that you learn from it and get better.

But that wasn't the only wakeup call we would experience over the next few months. We were winning against mediocre out-of-conference foes, but we were just playing well enough to grab a victory. There was not a dominance being displayed that indicated what this team was fully capable of. And things were not looking up. In Texas, we laid an egg inside the Dallas Cowboys Stadium, scoring sixty-two points. We only lost by five, but to an average Baylor team that allowed for no decent excuse for our defeat. It was the kind of loss that put us into a stupor and the kind of game that was a breaking point in the coach and player conflict.

Every year I had been at Kentucky, there had always been a battle between Coach Cal and the players that goes unseen by the fans. The great thing about the Cal philosophy is that there is never a shortage of talent to work with. He said this in a press conference once addressing the Big Blue Nation, perfectly encapsulating the strategy he uses and giving his secret to success.

"You need three things to win a championship with your basketball team. The first thing you need to have: great players. Once you've got that, there's another element you need to add to ensure your victory, which is this: great players. And after you have both of those things, there's one thing left to make sure you cut down those nets: players that are great."

He has certainly done that every year he has been a coach. The dark side of the coin is that with great players come great egos. And with great egos come great chances of selfishness, immaturity, and disunity. I do not envy the job it must be to collaborate every fresh batch of all-stars into one cohesive unit that shares the ball, plays tenacious defense, and looks after their brothers on the court. With great players come the great and inevitable storm not of team versus the opponents but of team versus coach. There is usually that one definable instance during the season when Coach was not getting the caliber of play that he was looking for from the team, and he made sure we are aware of this in ways that are all but subtle. In return, we became angry with him and basically shut down any function that had to do with listening.

For this particular season, that game against Baylor was the boiling point of tempers and egos. Following the game, there was an unusual circumstance that Mother Nature added to our punishment. After an embarrassing loss and a good reaming from the coaches, there was an ice storm that delayed our flight for almost twenty-four hours, preventing us from getting back to Lexington. Yes, an ice storm in Texas. Of course, the intercession of the coaches must have reached the basketball gods because somehow they managed to get a flight back home, leaving us to fend for ourselves back in Dallas for the day. Normally, a day to ourselves in a hotel would've been a nice perk, but we had descended into a slump of negativity after our performance, and then we were left behind like a group of pitiable orphans. Some knew that if they could ride out the storm, they'd be adopted by the NBA in about a year and come into a rich inheritance. Others couldn't lean on that certainty, especially after the way we played as a team. Either way, we were a house divided, on and off the court, a group of young men who desperately needed each other but were hard-wired to rely on no one. In this state of disunity, it seemed that the easiest way to build a common bond was to unify against a common enemy.

In a secluded room, we had lunch together, followed by a two-hour session featuring an activity that a group of nineteen- to twenty-one-year-old boys rarely engage in. We talked.

As I listened to the comments, part of me was reminded of the fact that I had been in those exact shoes, with my feet held closer to the fire, and I survived. I had made it through to the other side of the suffering, stood my ground, and received the reward of perseverance after my third year. As a senior leader, this was my chance to take the conversation away from where it was going and share my wisdom, experience, and the message that if we learned the right lessons about ourselves, the end of the season could be drastically different than what we felt in that moment.

But I didn't say any of those things. This is not an example of Jarrod Polson in his perfect moment when he used his spiritual enlightenment to guide his fellow teammates into a constructive and redemptive perspective. This is the moment when I reveal that I, too, am born of woman and make my share of mistakes. I said none of those things, and instead of curbing the discussion, I joined in on the roast. I fed the fire like you wouldn't believe, allowing my emotions of being in the "playing time doghouse" to control the way that I behaved. I am not proud of that day, but I am thankful that the coaches' vanishing act was not all part of some covert scheme to bug the hotel and listen in to what we had to say in their absence. Had that been the case, I never would have been taken out of the doghouse.

Here's the thing about Coach Cal. I can tell stories about our players only meetings and remarks about him because he knows exactly what goes on behind closed doors. If you ask any player that has ever played under Cal, they will undoubtedly tell you that there were moments where they couldn't stand him. But that's what makes Coach so special and successful. He values the development and success of his players over his own reputation or if his feelings are going to be hurt. This character trait is rare, but extremely admirable, and is a huge reason why every player also looks back and talks about their love for Coach Cal and the sacrifices he made for them. Coach may be tough on us at times, but he's man enough to do the necessary things to improve not only our skills but our character.

As it was, the year continued on, and as long as the general attitude on the team was one of self-pity and blame, we continued to spiral in the wrong direction. You may remember the loss we had to Arkansas in the Razorbacks' lair. It's hard to forget a game when you lose on a last-second, emphatically nasty dunk tip. We thought the game was over, so there was no need to block out. Blocking out is for unathletic sissies who have to work for their victories. And you would think that loss would have changed everything for us. Not the case. We ended up losing three out of four games to end the season. Time had run out for us to figure out how do things on our own, and the individual efforts to lean on self-sufficiency rather than teamwork and humility were slowly killing what could have been a championship team.

We were desperate, and as everyone knows, desperate times call for desperate measures... like, say, loving your enemies? My individual journey with forgiveness had taught me a great deal about the power of loving an "enemy," and now it was time for the team as a whole to learn a similar lesson. We were hungry to prove that this team had something special to offer, that all the hype at the beginning of the year wasn't just silly rhetoric, but we were totally lost and defeated. By this point we knew that if we really wanted to win, the time had come to put away the egos and change the attitudes. What mattered was whether or not we would trust in what Coach told us to do—and not only hear what he said but actually do it. I think there's a Bible verse about that.

Right before the SEC tournament, we had the opportunity to give this new perspective a chance. Coach Cal gave us a few tweaks that would help us out as we tried to forget about the losses of the season and focus on what was ahead. This tweak became a media hit, some mystery that couldn't be understood by the fans and was gold for the commentators and newspapers. Here's a spoiler alert for you: the tweak was not genius, mysterious, or complicated. It was this simple: "Andrew, get as many assists as you can. Julius, be the garbage man. Get every rebound, tip, and put back. That's how you score. Quit worrying about your offensive game."

This sounds like a staple speech given by a middle school dad during halftime. And yet, Coach Cal's simple yet genius trick somehow did it again, and this tweak brought about ridiculous change in this team. Suddenly Andrew Harrison started getting his head up and looking to pass before he shot, opening up all kinds of possibilities on offense. There was a defining moment when Randle was charging the hoop and did his trademark spin, but he wound up picking up his dribble, completely trapped by a double team. During the regular season, Julius would've forced a shot anyway because it's the only thing his brain allowed him to do in his self-sufficient beast mode. But in this moment you could see the light bulb explosion as he paused and realized that if all five players were swarming him in the paint, that must mean Aaron Harrison was open on the three-point line. And he passed the ball, which was immediately followed by three-point harp music.

These two bits of advice opened up a gateway into a whole new team, and we looked like a group of young men on a mission. We made it to the SEC championship and lost to an incredible Florida team by only one point. But it was the kind of loss we could celebrate because we knew we could have had that game and there was a momentum building in the right direction. We may have lost, but that couldn't take away the fact that there was a something brewing in our unit that was going to be magical, like some sort of fire being made within us.

And the so-called tweak gained all sorts of continued buzz, even though the reality was that it was painfully simple. It wasn't the complexity or mystery that made it special. It was the simple fact that we made the choice to trust Cal regardless of our feelings and do what he told us. That's it. And when we gave up the right to bitterness and self-pity, amazing things started to happen.

During the NCAA tournament, we were put into the most difficult bracket and started the journey as an eight seed. We didn't care. We were fired up. We rolled over Kansas State in the first round, and the nation got to see the joyous celebration at the end. By now we had learned to celebrate each other and took joy in each other's accomplishments. We were all smiles. Of course, the next game would bring us up against the overall one seed, who hadn't lost a game all season: Wichita State. Earlier in the year people thought that would be us, and now we were facing them as a lowly eight seed, maybe the most hilariously dubbed underdog team in the history of college basketball. And this game turned out to be one for the ages. The emotions of both teams and the fans were off the charts, and the battle was intense from start to finish. I only played five minutes in that game, but afterward I was absolutely exhausted. But after edging out Wichita State with just a two-point victory, the hype of old was back in full swing as the number one seed of the tournament had just fallen to the preseason number one.

Great as that victory was, the destination was far from reached. The next game was going to be Louisville in the sweet sixteen. Could it have been better scripted? The fierce rivalry there ended with a bang worthy of the competitive tradition, as the magic of Aaron Harrison began. He turned clutch three-point buzzer beaters into the status quo, performing that normal day's work against Louisville, Michigan, and Wisconsin. After that, it began to feel as though this team was destined to win a championship after all. Of course, UCONN had been developing their own magical story on the other side of the bracket. Still, we were very confident going into this final game, fully confident we would win.

———

The night before the big game, I was far too antsy to fall asleep, and I stumbled across a Jeremy Lin documentary, showing his life story and how he went from a no name D-League player to leading the New York Knicks to a winning record. I couldn't help but be inspired by this, and that night as I lay in bed looking up at heaven, I had a few requests. I was begging that I might have my own breakout play during this final championship game for the team that I loved. And ultimately, I prayed that we might just pull off the final victory.

Unfortunately, the next day, it turned out that neither of my prayers would be answered. I didn't even get to play at all in the game, and we lost. Of course, I could forever spin the story so that my lack of playing was the cause for our loss. By this point, though, I'm not sure I could have made my story any better with another chance to prove myself to the world. Besides, I understood as a senior that the most important thing about the season was not how I played but how the team did. And in this moment was the despair of utter defeat. All the magic of our run, all the energy and emotion that we had put into basketball and into the dream we had, and we had failed. In the blink of an eye, everything vanished, and we had nothing to show for it.

However, the truth is, I'm not sure Kentucky needed to hang the ninth banner in Rupp Arena as another reminder of how talent is king over all. Maybe we weren't destined to win. Maybe we were destined to learn through the loss. I had come to understand through my career at Kentucky that I couldn't and shouldn't be defined by my talent, and the team had learned this as well. We were forged with talent, but we were refined by adversity and finally began to excel when we made selfless choices and cared more about each other than personal success.

Even though I had won a national championship two years before and tasted what it was like to own a ring, I had more fun in the year that we lost the championship game. We had been through more together. We had learned about forgiveness and how to love our enemies. We had lost our hope of a deep tournament run, only to have it revived when we started playing like a team as the tweak did its work. There was no tweak, but there was love.

When I was finally able to see from this perspective, life got a whole lot more meaningful. The way we normally keep score versus what actually constitutes a win or a loss are very different gauges. The Bible mentions actually being thankful for the things that are difficult, the setbacks, or the weaknesses, the trials, the insults, and the hardships. That sounds crazy, impossible, and out of touch with the gloomy world we live in. But the perspective must be grounded in the knowledge of the one who made the world since trust in Him means that the tragedies we encounter don't actually constitute the final score. We know that individual losses will mean little when compared to the total victory found in Jesus. There are days when I might lose perspective and blame God for not answering the way I would have liked or cushioning my circumstances the way I think I deserve or making Himself known like I think would be most beneficial. But I've got to let go of that blame, of that bitterness, and begin to trust Him again. If I can stop focusing on the circumstances I *think* I need, I will realize the blessings I already have that are eternally more significant than whatever trinket I would seek in comparison.

When I look on my four years at UK, my senior year wild ride will be something I cherish more than winning a championship. We didn't attain everything we wanted that year, but as a team realized that there were more important things than championships. We gave the Big Blue Nation an exciting run that will never be forgotten, regardless of the final outcome. I do not recall the final score of that game. What I can't help but recall is the relationships formed throughout the season. Neither will I have trouble recalling the timeless truth of what can happen when you choose to replace selfishness with love and hatred with forgiveness.

My time at the University of Kentucky is something I will cherish forever. The journey certainly had bumps in the road, but I do not want to take away the wonderful memories and lessons learned throughout my four year tenure. I know that I have become a better man, and I am not quite sure where I would be if I hadn't chosen the path to walk on to my favorite college in the world. I am forever grateful to the University, the coaches, the UK Athletics Staff, and everyone else involved who have molded me into the person I am today. The program and the fans accepted me with wide open arms, and I can't express how lucky and blessed I feel because of that. People ask me all the time if I am glad I chose to play at Kentucky. In my mind, the question doesn't need to be answered. The way I have been treated and taken in by the program is unlike anything I ever imagined. Choosing to play for the Cats was one of the best decisions I have ever made and I will dearly hold on to every memory.

— 16

Living Beyond the Dream

If you look for truth, you may find comfort in
the end; if you look for comfort you will not get
either comfort or truth, only soft soap and wishful
thinking to begin, and in the end, despair.
—C. S. Lewis

During my four years at Kentucky, I had the opportunity to do, see, and hear so many things that it feels impossible to find the perfect scene to wrap up my story in a nice pretty bow. So I figured I would leave you with the phrase that I heard repeated more than anything else during my tenure: "Living the dream."

"Hey, man, how's everything going? You're living the dream, aren't ya!"

"Good game last night! Living the dream, huh?"

"Man, what I would give to be in your shoes ... you're living every Kentucky boy's dream!"

When I had these interactions, almost on a daily basis, I would always smile and acknowledge the truth of these statements. After all, what kid doesn't grow up wishing to play a game for a living as long as life will let him? And I know that all of these people meant well and were trying to pay me a compliment. But after my smile faded and the person walked away, there was something of an uneasy feeling in my gut. In my mind, this phrase has always carried with it a negative connotation because your dream is meant to be your lifeblood. A dream is meant to be your true north, the all-encompassing ambition on which your desires rise and set. And while playing basketball at UK was an awesome thing I got to do, it's not where my greatest satisfaction is found.

Plus, the word *dream* itself has become synonymous, at least in my mind, with the phrase *American dream*. That's something we all learn about from a young age, and it involves the usual list of manmade accomplishments. Some people really want to get a good job and make a lot of moolah so they can have power, or at least die with the most toys. Others focus more on getting married and having a family, complete with 2.2 children, a white picket fence, and a Labrador retriever named Marley. (And we all know how that ends.) Then others dream about rampant success and fame by hoping to become professional athletes, actors, or musicians. Or you just dream about being Shaquille O'Neil, so you can have it all at once. But regardless of the dream, they all have a common thread, which is an end result of being comfortable and happy. And at a surface level, these two aspirations aren't harmful, since the human being needs some level of both to survive. The trouble is, often there is an ingredient mixed in with these ambitions that leads to a person's eventual downfall. Here's what I am getting at:

Most of us are taught from an early age to be selfish. And as you have gotten older, think about the advice you have received when it comes to your future and the goals you're striving for. I'm sure at some point you've heard something like this: "Do what is best for you."

This comes up in athletics constantly, which is ironic simply because individual athletes are the things that make up a team. The decisions of what college to attend, if you're going to stay another year or go straight to the pros, how you should spend your money, or what to do with your free time—all these forks in the road receive plenty of justification from the school of thought that says, "Look out for you."

In America, we have taken selfish ambition and made it sexy. And we wonder why we have so many problems. Why can't we have peace? Why is there still hunger? Why are people still bought and sold? We ask these questions, which seem so obviously wrong, and yet we are blind to our unapologetic worship of the self-goddess. But rather than accept the finger of blame, we turn it outward at entities that feel so good to hate. Unfortunately, the world would not be fixed if we could annihilate the liberal Democrats or conservative Republicans. Our problems would not be solved if we could just determine a winner between radical Presbyterians or legalistic Baptists. The world would not be perfect if we found the cure for cancer or increased life expectancy to one thousand years. Pain would still be here even if we elected the perfect president or invented a calorie-free ice cream. This earth still wouldn't be heaven if we abolished all crime or perfected time travel. Whether it's because of our own fallen condition, how we are raised, or the spiritual forces at work, the world has been duped into believing that our lives are our own, to do with them whatever is best for us as individuals.

But before I take the finger of blame and keep it pointed out there, or at you who sit and read these words, allow me to have my own confession. The problem is *ours* because the problem is also *mine*. It's easy to sit behind a keyboard and write about the mysteries of life and their solutions and quite another to be held responsible to those ideals. I have claimed to understand these truths my entire life, and I can send out tweets about how you need to live your life as a sacrifice for God, but that doesn't mean I have arrived at the destination. I have failed so many times and make selfish decisions just as much as the next guy. You've already read about some of them. There were times when the team needed my leadership, needed me to use my voice to bring the right perspective. Instead I used my words to increase gossip, to let us sink further into negativity because I wasn't getting what I wanted. There were times when I felt incredible emotion about the injustice of having my basketball number taken, and on that same day, I didn't have a single thought about over one million pre-born American babies this year alone whose chances at experiencing life were taken away before they even got to breathe a breath of fresh air. There were obviously times when I cared more about becoming a superstar than about loving people in my life. I, too, have worshiped at the feet of the self-goddess, so please don't picture me in a pulpit speaking down at you. I am a fellow sojourner on the same playing field as you, searching just like you are for an answer to all of this.

I do know that guilt and shame are not the answers. When we start to ponder sin and selfishness, the easiest thing to do is run and hide or at least cover up our evils with a life that looks pretty good to the world. But the good news is, we don't have to do either. We can't run from God, and we can't cover the wrongs we've done or the selfishness in our souls by doing a bunch of good works. It wouldn't work, and even better, there's no need to. Jesus came to pay for our sins with His death so we could be forgiven and experience His life. The problem with so much of our thinking about God is the same problem in our thinking about dreams. We're obsessed with what we can do to fix things and give us ultimate happiness. No dream we work for will fix our souls, and nothing we do to work for God's forgiveness will ever make us right in front of a perfect Creator. I know some of you reading this are thinking, *Here we go ... the Jesus thing ... I've heard this a thousand times.* But don't tune me out. If I tell you a story, you have to listen. Everybody loves stories.

So I was talking with my friend Blake, and we decided to pray together with a few other guys from Christian Student Fellowship. We figured that if God was really there, and we were trying to get His attention, we'd have a better chance of doing that if we joined forces. We did something that a lot of guys might think is weird, but we prayed together. We listened in silence on behalf of each other, waiting to see if God would tell us anything. We weren't really anticipating an audible voice but were aiming to hear a whisper in our hearts that we knew was from above. Suddenly Blake broke the silence and started praying for me out loud, and he said something I will never forget.

"Jarrod, God told me to tell you that His favorite moments with you are at night when you're sitting up in your bed and talking to Him."

That simple sentence probably didn't mean much to Blake, but it contained words I will hold on to forever. Two things struck me from what he said. The first was the simple fact that Blake had no idea that I liked to sit in bed at night and pray, which gave me confidence that the words were truly not his own. He really was relaying a divine telegram. And second, the message that he was delivering was like water to my soul. I have lived most of my life as someone whose identity is mainly comprised by basketball. It's what I did in most of my free time, and it's the thing people wanted to talk to me about in their free time. My family played basketball together on Sundays when we were growing up, and now as a college student, random people I didn't know at all would come up and talk to me because I played basketball at Kentucky. People who know absolutely nothing about what kind of person I am will come up to me in public places and have me sign a piece of paper because of the jersey I borrowed from the school for the last four years. If you Google me, you will see that I am a UK basketball player. So if my heavenly Father was going to send me a message to communicate how proud He was of me, Blake would have said something like the following: "Jarrod, God told me to tell you that He is still getting goose bumps over that Maryland game."

"Jarrod, God said that He is really proud of your commitment to purity. He realizes you could have thousands of illegitimate children across the state of Kentucky, but you're saving yourself until marriage. Keep it up."

"Jarrod. You are white, but you can dunk. I'm not sure what happened there. Could I get your autograph? Actually, could you sign three of these? Gotta keep things fair up here."

"Jarrod, I made you a baller. And when you swish threes, you should feel My pleasure."

"Jarrod, before I knit you together in your mother's womb, I knew you'd be on Kentucky's team. However, I didn't think Calipari would ever play you. Nicely done."

"Jarrod, you have more NBA contacts in your phone than David Stern. Can I get Anthony Davis's number?"

See, I assumed that God would be enamored with who I became for the same reason that everyone else seemed enamored. But in that moment of Blake's modest revelation, I was lambasted with this profound truth: God loves me for who I am—not for what I can do and not for what I haven't done. I was simply amazed at how radically this affected my self-worth. The pressure was gone, my identity was forged, and for once in my life, I knew without a doubt who I was—not what I could do but who I was. And that was the best drink of water I ever tasted.

———

I think that beneath all of our dreams is one that is absolutely universal for all of humanity, and that is the desire to have a father who is proud of us. We want a dad who will celebrate us in our victories but also fight for us when we are defeated. And this is exactly what God has done for us in Jesus Christ. He is proud of who we are, so much that even though we failed Him in our rebellion, He fought for us through the death of His Son. God didn't send Jesus down to this earth to create a religion called Christianity. He sent His Son to save you, me, and this world from our selfish and sinful selves.

I know there are so many people who struggle with their definitions of themselves revolving around bad things they've done or can't stop doing or things they wish they could do but can't. God doesn't see any of those things. He sees you as His child, and His favorite part of the day would be the part where you don't do anything except sit there and talk to Him.

For me, this lightbulb moment made a lot of sense as I looked back on my time at UK. I experienced some incredible things according to the world's standards, like three final four trips and a national championship. But looking back, my top memories would not be winning it all or stroking a three in Rupp Arena or even the Maryland game. My best memories were directly related to the things Jesus said were the best: loving the Lord with all your heart, mind, and soul, and loving your neighbor as yourself. Stooping with my best friends on Kalmia, praying with people close to me, playing Mancala with my little sister Alyse, or going to Ethiopia and handing out bread to hungry people and seeing their selfless response—I will take those and give up the championship ring any day of the week. A lot of people may wonder why I'm not choosing to keep playing basketball overseas or do something crazy like praying for Jeremy Lin round two and trying out for an NBA team. But the truth is, I'm just tired. I'm tired of working so hard to climb the success ladder and worrying about how far my talent can take me in this life. *I have seen that the powers of talent don't compare to the power of our choices.* And for now, I am choosing a different path.

———

After graduating I had the opportunity to go on a trip to Israel, Rome, and Greece with a group from church to visit the actual places I've grown up reading of in the Bible. The experience was incredible, and there were too many lessons to learn and places to see for those poor two weeks that were crammed full of action. One place in Rome keeps revisiting my mind and sticking out among the other memories. It was the place where Paul was supposedly martyred for his faith. There were fifty feet of stones in somewhat of an ancient sidewalk that were blocked off from the rest to signify Paul's final steps. According to tradition, this somber segment is where Paul took his last fifty steps before being beheaded by the Romans. It was a heavy place to witness, and it was odd how staring at the place of Paul's death could make me think so much about his life. He was so engrossed in sharing the good news about Jesus that he didn't care what happened to him. The threat of death was no surprise, and yet he was so passionate that it didn't make any difference. He trusted God and had faith—a faith so strong that even in the face of death he never doubted God's goodness. He had all sorts of cause to complain about his lot in life, after so many beatings, so much ridicule, so much imprisonment, and yet his memory is one of complete joy in the face of suffering. He wrote these words: "Therefore, I urge you, brethren, by the mercies of God, to present your bodies as a living and holy sacrifice, acceptable to God, which is your spiritual act of worship" (Romans 12:1).

I want my life to be like Paul's. And I have no idea how many steps I have left. I just know that if I only have fifty, I don't really want to spend them playing basketball in Europe solely to make more money and prove to the world that I'm a good basketball player. Of course, I have to be careful. Paul was the kind of person whose ideals matched his life. He was actually willing to give up his life for Jesus, in a completely metaphorical and literal way, showing an example of self-sacrifice. I think we would all look more like Paul, and more importantly Jesus, if we knew the secret they stored in their hearts while they were on this earth. This secret is the simple fact that they knew their purpose in life: to worship God and love people. But not only did they *know* it, they reminded themselves enough to be able to *live* it. Sometimes we need to take a step back from our work, from school, from making money, from our reputations, from our hobbies, and from athletics and remind ourselves of why we are really on this earth. All of those things may be necessary, but they should always point toward and aid our true purpose.

It's one thing to look up to someone like Paul and another thing altogether to seek to be like him. We get jazzed up when we see a movie or hear a story about people sacrificing themselves for others. Movies like *American Sniper* and *Lone Survivor* evoke a holy spark in our hearts because they are unbelievably inspiring examples of the highest love. We say that God is hard to find in our world today and that Jesus doesn't do miracles anymore. And then we cry when we hear a story when someone is heroic enough to give up his or her own life to allow another to live. Those tears are a reminder from our Father in heaven that His love hasn't gone anywhere, and it can be unleashed in us when we choose to surrender. Jesus said, "If anyone wishes to come after me, he must deny himself, and take up his cross and follow me. For whoever wishes to save his life will lose it; but whoever loses his life for my sake will find it" (Matthew 16:24–25).

Anyone who has ever lost a family member to military combat knows of the simultaneous grief and pride they have in the sacrifice of their loved one. When someone dies to preserve the life of

someone else, they are giving the world a glimpse of agape love—
the most powerful force on this planet.

———

It's time for me, and for us, to stop *talking* about this kind of love and
start *living* it out—to stop pursuing the dreams that will make us
happy and be willing to give up our lives for the happiness of others.
I think this is where the testimony of Christians in my lifetime and
generations before me has failed. As Ghandi said, "I like your Christ; I
don't like your Christians. Your Christians are so unlike your Christ."
This is a tragedy that can only be fixed by the church. I have gone to
church my whole life, and I fully admit that the danger is we have
tried so hard to fit in with everyone and be so "appealing" that we have
actually become unappealing in the process. And for that, we, and I,
should be sorry. No one has ever wanted to become a Christ follower
because someone said, "Hey, you can have fun as a Christian too."
People aren't looking for a new way to have fun. There are drugs for
that. People are looking for something *real* that can genuinely change
their lives. And that's Jesus. As long as we are too busy chasing our
dreams and not displaying something real, then people have no reason
to turn away from their substitutes of alcohol, drugs, sex, video games,
whatever. I need to show the way. We need to show the way—not just
with words but with actions. Another friend of mine named Curt also
traveled with me to the Middle East, and God spoke some convicting
words into his heart on this truth: "The kingdom of power is coming
to wage war on the kingdom of talk."

First Corinthians 4:20 seems to agree with this: "For the
Kingdom of God is not a matter of talk but of power."

The good news is that this power doesn't have to come from
us; in fact, it can't. The do-it-yourself mentality will only leave you
feeling guilty and ashamed, always trying to earn grace, a gift that
has already been freely given.

Philippians 2:13 says, "For it is God who works in you to will and to act in order to fulfill his good purpose."

God promises that the Holy Spirit will be released into our souls when we accept Him, giving us the desires that will ultimately lead to good works. I have seen so many people who try Christianity for a time, only to discover that they simply can't live a holy life on their own. And so they resort right back to the very things that left them empty and hollow. But if I am being honest, I still sometimes play the game of religiosity. So many times I have tried to "be good" on my own, trying to follow the rules that every Christian should abide by. And other times, I have used grace as a cop-out, excusing my sins or lack of good works because of the gift I have received. The timeless debate between grace and works has been an internal battle for Christians throughout history, but I am beginning to see a more simplistic answer.

John 15:4 states, "Remain in me, as I also remain in you. No branch can bear fruit by itself; it must remain in the vine. Neither can you bear fruit unless you remain in me."

Instead of trying to do good things to earn grace, I need to learn to accept grace first, and when I do, that's when the fruit shows up. I must remain in Christ, leaning on the power of the Holy Spirit instead of my own faulty human nature, giving my entire existence to the only one who can completely change my desires and transform them into a life of grace acceptance and selfless love.

———

It is time for the kingdom of power to be unleashed in my life—not the talent I have to play basketball and make money but for the love of Jesus to be accepted into my heart and given away to the world. Jon Weece, pastor of Southland Christian Church, recently wrote a book called *Jesus Prom* and his subtitle simply states, "Life gets fun when you love people like God does." I am beginning to see the truth of this statement. It took me a long time to realize that my dream is small potatoes compared to the dreams God has for me. I may not have seen any outrageous miracles, but I believe they do happen. God still cures diseases, saves lives, and speaks to people in powerful ways. But every miracle begins with a changed heart from someone who realizes his or her dreams are futile compared to the reality of God's love and grace. Once that miracle occurs, we can walk out in faith and discover what miraculous happenings will follow. So it's time for a new dream—not the dream I have to ensure my happiness and comfort and my name on a jersey. It might not guarantee the longest and most comfortable possible life, but it does promise the best one.

Afterword

As my basketball career has come to an end, I am faced with an odd but exciting time in my life. In my twenty-three years of living, the nature of school and basketball has placed on me a life of following orders from coaches, teachers, and parents. It is a weird feeling to be completely on my own, now having the privilege of making my own decisions and figuring out what to do with the rest of my life. Since I have graduated with degrees in finance and marketing, I have been able to travel around the state of Kentucky and meet a ton of the fans. I've spoken to many schools and churches about my time as a UK basketball player and the lessons I learned while doing it. I have also been able to travel to a few different countries, including Israel, Greece, Rome, and the Dominican Republic. I currently work for Kentucky Nonprofit Funds and am getting started with Remix Education as well. I hope to get more involved with different nonprofits, such as FCA, Upward, Score International, Operation UNITE, etc. Living Beyond the Dream is the title of this book, but my goal is that this is just a launch pad for future basketball camps, speaking opportunities, school assemblies, and much more. My ultimate hope is that I will be able to use the influence I have from playing for my dream school to encourage and challenge people of all ages to live beyond their dreams.